Sacred Grit
Faith to Push Through When You Feel like Giving Up

John D. Duncan

Austin Brothers Publishing
Fort Worth, Texas

© 2015 by John D. Duncan

Sacred Grit:
Faith to Push Through When You Feel like Giving Up
by John D. Duncan
ISBN 978-0-9903477-9-8

Published by Austin Brothers Publishing
Fort Worth, Texas
www.austinbrotherspublishing.com

Printed in the United States of America

All rights reserved. No part of this publication may be reproduced, stored in a retrival system, or transmitted in any form or by any means—for example, electronic, photocopy, recording—without the prior written permission of the publisher. The only exception is brief quotations in printed reviews.

This and other books published by Austin Brothers Publishing can be purchased at www.austinbrotherspublishing.com

Contents

Introduction   1

Sacred Fear   27

Sacred Agony   83

Sacred Sweat   139

Foreword

After a 17 year coaching career I believe I am qualified to say a few words about this word *grit*. It is often a term associated with athletics. Almost every coach has witnessed the best and the worst examples of those who have exemplified and portrayed grit, and of course those who have not.

In either case, tremendous lessons have been learned. Society spends a great deal of time extolling the virtues of those whom have overcome adversity. Many of these individuals and teams have gone on to become champions in chosen fields.

Just recently at the Texas State High School Track and Field Championships, Charlotte Brown from Rains High School finished third in the girls pole vault, winning her first medal in her third year at state. What makes this event so special? Charlotte is legally blind. This is the epitome of grit.

Our society has also vilified those from all walks of life who have wasted talents on steroids, drugs, alcohol and lustful ego-driven behaviors. These are easily identifiable. The media will not allow us to forget either of these groups.

In his book *Sacred Grit*, Dr. John Duncan digs even deeper into this notion of grit. We often fashion grit to be defined as determination or guts. But, *Sacred Grit* goes beyond the scope of our day-to-day descriptions of perseverance or determination.

In Romans 5:3-4 the apostle Paul writes, "And not only that, but we also glory in tribulations, knowing that tribulation produces perseverance; and perseverance character; and character hope."

While Paul extols the virtues of going through trials and tribulations, we don't necessarily enjoy difficult journeys. *Sacred Grit* helps us to see what God would have us learn during such trials.

Dr. Duncan provides us with a glimpse of what true grit means through the eyes of an athlete, a farmer, and a soldier. While I have been an athlete I have never been a farmer, but my table has been blessed with the bounty of their handiwork. Neither have I served in the military but I have enjoyed the freedom and liberty afforded to me because of the great sacrifice of those willing to serve. Dr. J captures the essence of determination and perseverance of these groups in *Sacred Grit*.

Sacred grit should produce the virtues of mercy and grace in each of us. This is indeed the type of grit we should desire. In his book *Sacred Grit,* Dr. Duncan provides examples of how we too can persevere through difficult times. The gifts from sacred grit proffered through difficult times were not simply given to John Duncan. He has earned them.

Dr. Duncan is an outstanding author, preacher, and pastor. More importantly, he is a great friend. He exhibits the grace of Christ in his daily walk, and he inspires us to follow his lead. *Sacred Grit* teaches us how to walk this path. May God bless you on the journey.

Dr. Charles Breithaupt
Executive Director
University Interscholastic League
Co-Author of *King Cotton*

Introduction

THE DUST COVERED THE STREETS, clung to clothes, and drifted like smoke billowing from an underground furnace on a city street. Actually, the dust combined as both fallen ashes wafting through the air like fog, and smoke filling the air like a burning trash pile in your back yard. A man searches for his son in the ashes and smoke, much like driving a car through fog on the Blue Ridge Parkway on a chilly, frosty morning in the mountains of North Carolina.

"Where am I?"

"What's coming?"

"What is ahead?"

"What might suddenly dart in front of me?"

"Where am I going?"

"Where have I been?"

"Can I get to where I am going?"

"When is the next round, sharp turn?"

"Is there a light at the end of the tunnel?"

As much as these appear as existential questions about life, driving through the dense fog in the mountains can feel tense, require strict attention to the details of turns, and white and yellow lines on the road, and push you to your emotional limits.

My friend searched for his son on a bicycle, asking another question, "Where is my son?"

His son had started his morning routine as casually as sipping a cup of coffee. He dressed. He grabbed his backpack. He took the subway, disembarked from the train, and arrived in time for class at the Stuyvesant High School. Like most high school students in 2001, he talked about high school stuff like homework, parents, girls, football, and music. One of the number one songs in September of 2001 held a simple title, *Fallin* by Alicia Keys.

My friend, Taylor, raced to the school amid falling ashes, falling debris, falling twin towers, falling dreams, falling hopes, and falling despair. Like the English singing song and nursery rhyme about *London Bridge is Falling Down*, it seemed, that New York, specifically Manhattan, was falling down, falling down...my fair lady.

The rhythmic meter, posed as a traditional nursery rhyme, was published in London in 1744. Also known as *My Fair Lady*, New York in dust appeared to be fallin and falling down, and there was not one thing beautiful like a lady or fair in any sense of the word happening on September 11, 2001 in New York City.

Chaos ensued. Sirens blared. Parents raced to find their children safe. At one point, the refuse, the trash, the fallen ash that had covered people, the ground, and the world with dust, became so thick that a police officer charged my friend Taylor to wash off the mess from his clothes. Taylor stood in a shower, clothes and all, wondering about the blank stares of people's faces, wondering if he would see his son's face again. Other people both wandered and wondered since that day about another thing: the Face of God.

In life, most of us find ourselves pinched between the Psalmist's cries, albeit desperate pleas: "Do not hide your face from your servant; answer me quickly, for I am in trouble" (Psalm 69:17, NIV), and "May God be gracious to us and bless us and make his face shine upon us" (Psalm 67:1, NIV). We cry out in despair for God to remove the curse of trouble. We plead with God to shine his light on us. We find ourselves surrounded by ash, dust, and the grittiness of the unpleasant. We find ourselves longing for hope, for renewed cleansing, a shower that cleanses the heart, and a breakthrough that makes life fresh and livable again.

I asked Taylor to describe in one word his experience of September 11, of probing the darkness while looking for his son, and of remembering the trauma of terror on a sunlit day that hijacked the city and his heart of darkness.

Numbness, he replied as simply and quietly as a woman knitting a blanket for her grandbaby in the stillness of the fresh morning hours.

"A gentle heart is tied with an easy thread," the seventeenth-century English parson, priest, and poet George Herbert once wrote.[1] But what do you do when the thread unravels, frays to the point of breaking, or actually tears apart into two pieces? What do you do in life when life's thread unravels, and you can barely hang on? When life frays and you are not sure you can survive much longer? When life breaks at the most inopportune or unexpected time, and sends your life in two directions at once?

---

1 George Herbert, *The Complete English Works* (London: Alfred A. Knopf, 1995), 278.

Does the heart move from gentle to hard in the aftermath? Does the heart surrender hope? Does the heart break and grieve as never to recover, never to rise from the ashes so to speak, and tie a knot in the broken place to attempt to move forward, to try to weave life's happiness and joy again?

"Are the children okay? I clutched the policeman's arm. Everyone's been evacuated safely, he said. I asked four other people just to make sure." Taylor penned those words in his book *Mercy Streets: Seeing Grace on the Streets of New York*.[2]

A police officer turned Taylor away that day. Amid piles of dust, his emotions having fallen, risen, and catapulted his soul toward numbness, he pushed through the dust, found his way home, and waited. The wait ended with a phone call. His son Freeman phoned.

Later Freeman made it home with his entire football team who had nowhere to go. Pizza filled hungry stomachs, and pain swelled in empty hearts. Glad reunions seldom exceed the

---

[2] Taylor Field, *Mercy Streets: Seeing Grace on the Streets of New York* (Nashville, Tennessee: Broadman and Holman Publishers, 2003), 111. This story was adapted from Chapter 17, "The Dust of Death," pages 107-118. The response to my question about how he felt ("numbness") is used by permission.

happiness and joy of a prodigal who returns home, a lost son wondrously found, and pizza shared as a festive feast of friends like the fatted calf served in a banquet of joy and renewal, shared by Jesus in his story of the prodigal son.

After September 11, relief moved into some homes ("I found my son!" "My son was lost and now is found!"). Grief took residence in other hearts ("I lost my daughter!" "Oh, Absalom, Absalom, would that I had died and not you!"). Confusion raced and swirled through the town ("I can't find my wife!" "Have you seen my husband?" "Where is my son? Daughter?").

Posters with pictures plastered on walls, in subway passages, and tied to chain link fences, begged, "Have you seen this missing person?" Disaster gave way to happiness for people like Taylor and his wife Susan. Tragedy struck in dark shadows of grief for others. For most, at some level, anguish, anger, and angst resulted. Trauma set in. Coping resources were drilled like water wells. Classes on grief, trauma, and coping became the norm all over the city.

As I write these words, I think of John Donne (1572-1631). Donne was born into the home of a wealthy London merchant. He attended

university at Oxford, then Cambridge, but never graduated from either. He studied law, inherited his father's estate, wrote poetry, and ventured into adventures in Italy and Spain. Later, the Anglican Church ordained him. He served a brief stint in jail for marrying a minor, his wife Anne More. His marriage violated both common and cannon law. A writer, a poet, and a priest, he later took office in Saint Paul's Cathedral in London.

Donne's life swirled with turmoil and grief. Aside from landing in prison for a short time, he lost a job, once described his home life as a prison, faced insurmountable debt, struggled emotionally with a daily conflict in his soul, and agonized in recurring ill health. In a strange way, these torments heightened his pain, ignited his creativity, and opened the writer's vein to spill his creative blood in masterful strokes of pen and ink, poems of love, life, and satire.

In another strange twist of circumstances on January 23, 1615, sixteen years before his death, he took orders in the Anglican Church. Between 1625 and 1631, Donne became a masterful preacher whose passion drew large crowds. Amazingly, the attractive quality behind Donne's preaching lay in his ability to equip people with life skills: surviving life's troubles; coping with death; finding light in the darkness, and pushing through the hard things in life when people felt like giving up. In a word, Donne majored on helping people dig out of the dust of life and discover the new.

He wrote his infamous lines of poetry in a poem entitled *Nativitie*,

> *Batter my heart, three-person'd God; for you*
> *As yet but knocke, breathe, shine, and seeke to mend;*
> *That I may rise, and stand, o'erthrow mee,' and bend*
> *Your force, to breake, blow, burn, and make me new.*[3]

Donne preached at Saint Paul's Cathedral. He especially preached during a dark time in London, as dark as the days after September 11 in New York, during the plague. Historians record that approximately 40,000 people died because of the plague. Many people fled the city. During that time, Donne preached funeral after funeral.

---

3 John Donne, *Donne: Poems and Prose* (New York: Alfred A. Knopf, 1995), 164.

Donne's personal struggles and life experience of anguish supplied him with pastoral understanding and compassion.

His failures, "John Donne undone," as he once scribbled, equipped him with empathy and pathos. His sermons possessed a weathered quality: sometimes lightning and thunder in the flash of urgency for life; sometimes the gentle rain of God's misty comfort; and sometimes the glimmer of light shining with rays of hope into dark times on dark hearts wondering if ever they will see the light again.

One Sunday years ago, I entered Saint Paul's Cathedral in London on a Sunday night wishing to tour the cathedral, scale the lower steps into the basement to see the memorial to Donne, and view the massive, sacred space in its grandeur and aura.

I climbed the steps from the streets of London and walked through an open door. I walked into the cathedral in awe of its majesty and beauty. As I stood on the black and white checkered floor, I stared at the ornate artistry and craftsmanship in the vaulted architecture. A choir sang in echoes of glory, robed and singing while bystanders and attenders watched and worshipped. I listened, grabbed a program, heard the words in Latin, and looked at the program to see exactly what the choir was singing. They sang, "*Ubi caritas et amor, Ubi caritas Deus ibi est,*" that is, "Where charity and love, there is God."

Donne examined life and concluded, "No man is an island", that is, we need each other.[4] He also surmised in his *Devotions*, "Tribulation is treasure in the nature of it, but it is not current money in the use of it, except we get nearer and nearer, our home, heaven, by it."[5]

Donne agreed with Saint James, "Come near to God and he will come near to you. Wash your hands, you sinners, and purify your hearts, you double-minded. Grieve, mourn and wail. Change your laughter to mourning and your joy to gloom. Humble yourselves before the Lord, and he will lift you up" (James 4:8-10, NIV).

Donne appraises Paul's words as worthy of attaching to the heart, "Therefore, since we have been justified through faith, we have peace with God through our Lord Jesus Christ, through whom we have gained access by faith into this grace in which we now stand. And we rejoice in the hope of the glory of God. Not only so, but we also rejoice

---

4 Donne, *Donne: Poems and Prose*, 227.
5 Donne, *Donne: Poems and Prose*, 227.

in our sufferings, because we know that suffering produces perseverance; perseverance, character; and character, hope. And hope does not disappoint us, because God has poured out his love into our hearts by the Holy Spirit, whom he has given us" (Rom 5:1-5, NIV). Again Paul lauds, "I consider that our present sufferings are not worth comparing with the glory that will be revealed in us" (Romans 8:18).

Donne's poetic words, batter my heart, remind me that life pressures us, pummels us, and pushes us to the edge of the cliff. Donne's poem begs the question, Can we rediscover the new amid such battering? Can we live to feel refreshed again? Can we muster enough grit in the grief to find joy's grace? To discover afresh life's purpose? To glimpse a renewed sense of hope's glory?

Why have I told you Taylor' story? Why have I talked about John Donne? Because, in life, most of us find ourselves, at times, frantic, searching, covered in dust if you will, undone in suffering, uncomfortable in circumstances beyond reason, and unrelenting in places where life seems dim, dark, and hopeless. On the other hand, most of us find ourselves seeking calm, pursuing inner peace, trying to uncover from piles of dust and stuff, aiming to cope with suffering, wishing for better circumstances, and trying to move forward in life from those logger jams and unrelenting forces that try to paralyze us practically, and even spiritually.

Taylor's trauma and New York's tragedy required resolve, resiliency, will, and mechanisms for coping when life turned sour in terror angling toward renewed triumph. Donne's devotion sought renewal, a way to find pearls of treasure in life's dark moments, and a path down which to walk when the dust, fog, twists, and turns on life's mountain need to be navigated.

What I propose in this book, which New Yorkers have taught us in a sense, is sacred grit: pushing through when you feel like giving up. What I propose, like John Donne undone, but preaching hope in the dark hour, is sacred grit: pushing forward to find meaning's treasure, even in those painful experiences, which you never planned, anticipated, or expected.

Interestingly enough, if you read the book, *Resilience: The Science of Mastering Life's Greatest Challenges* (Cambridge University Press, 2012), written by two medical doctors, Doctors Southwick and Charney, they will tell you about

research developed after the September 11 disaster. In their book, they deliver good news in the bad, or ten keys to bouncing back from stress and trauma. The research uncovered the concept of resiliency.

The doctors note, "In the physical sciences, materials and objects are termed resilient if they assume their original shape upon being bent or stretched. In people, resilience refers to the ability to 'bounce back' after encountering difficulty."[6] These brilliant scholars discuss trauma, adversity, and disappointment, and their effects on the brain. They provide deep insight into cognitive skills, coping mechanisms, and drawing on faith in the face of fear, failure, and gaining a new sense of purpose.

They can tell you how the right, left, and other parts of the brain function, for example, the brain regions of the amygdala (alarm; fear), the prefrontal cortex (decisions, emotions, the executive center of the brain), and the hippocampus, so named because of its resemblance in shape to a "seahorse" (hippo, "horse," and campus, "sea

---

6 Steven M. Southwick and Dennis S. Charney, *Resilience: The Science of Mastering Life's Challenges* (Cambridge: Cambridge University Press, 2012), 7.

monster"), a part of the brain that influences memories.

The doctors and their research add understanding, for example, of the blind and handicapped Helen Keller's personal resolve, a veteran soldier's grit, and an athlete's training. It is the practice of resiliency in everyday life. Their interesting research, based on numerous interviews with people who faced fear, failure, the loss of a job, or cancer, or a traumatic event like September 11, highlights acceptance, an improved focus on moving past an event, and developing "the emotional stability to handle failure."[7]

I find the factor of gratitude one interesting aspect of their research. Adversity does not have to stop life's progress, but can push it forward and bear fruit such as gratitude. "I am thankful for what I went through," or "I am thankful I survived it," whatever "it" was, follows as sacred speech from those who demonstrated resiliency. In spiritual terms, a crisis handled in the shadow and cover of God's wings builds resiliency, gratitude if even in small doses, and trust in God's providence (Psalm 91).

---

7 Southwick and Charney, *Resilience: The Science of Mastering Life's Challenges*, 176.

One of the myths perpetuated in modern society indicates that successful people gain success by sheer determination, hard work, and over-achieving or out-doing their competition. Matthew Syed, in his book *Bounce*, reaffirms the myth of sheer talent and Malcolm Gladwell's ten years or practice and ten-thousand hour rule on the path to success.[8] Spend ten years and/or ten-thousand hours practicing a skill, a profession, or a gift/talent, and success follows.

Tennis star Roger Federer, hence the title *Bounce*, achieved tennis success through practice, a path toward excellence, and philosophical connections like optimism. Critics might say he bounced his way to the top of the tennis heap, or the ball bounced his way, so to speak. Syed says, "They (athletes, entrepreneurs, artists, and musicians) have taught themselves to ratchet up their optimism at the point of performance; to mold the evidence to fit their beliefs rather, than the other way around, to activate doublethink."[9] As the old adage goes, the body can achieve what the mind can believe.

---

8   Matthew Syed, *Bounce: The Myth of Talent and Power of Practice* (London: Fourth Estate, 2011), 15-16.

9   Syed, *Bounce: The Myth of Talent and Power of Practice*, 167.

Truthfully, though, each person has his or her limits, gifts, hopes, dreams, and disappointments. I like Syed's theory and his book, but even in triumphs there are falls, in successes failures, and in dreams achieved moments of despair. Did not Jesus utter wise words, "Therefore do not worry about tomorrow, for tomorrow will worry about itself. Each day has enough trouble of its own" (Matt 6:34, NIV)? Did not Jesus speak hopeful words in hapless world: "I have told you these things, so that in me you may have peace. In this world you will have trouble. But take heart! I have overcome the world" (John 16:33, NIV)?

Herein lies reality, we aim for success, long for dreams to come true, and achieve applause that makes the heart feel good, but sometimes trouble comes, dreams die, we stumble, fall, or even fail. In a word, our heads "bounce." Herein lies reality, we do worry, trouble arrives like an unwelcome guest, and the hapless world spins personal unhappiness. A rose also sticks on the stem with thorns. Mountains also descend into valleys. Light surrenders to darkness. In life, I must say, you cannot avoid thorns, valleys, or darkness. I guess you can learn to smell the roses, appreciate mountain views, and bask in the light.

But sometime, somewhere, in the chronology and history of your life, and Jesus put it best, you will have trouble. How do you respond? To whom do you turn in response?

We can read good books, like *The Resilience Factor*, and discover their seven keys to finding your inner strength and overcoming life's hurdles.[10] "Resilience matters" in handling stress, trauma, parenting skills, marriage trials, work challenges, debt, or a crisis. We can learn from the book good advice like how to bounce back when "shaken to the core," and that "life change is possible" by acknowledging and understanding your RQ, resilience quotient, with its accompanying coping skills.[11]

We can even read *Resilience And Why Things Bounce Back*, and process information, clusters, resources, and the steps to reorganize and reenergize life after an unforgettable and traumatic life event.[12] The authors put in clear terms thoughts

---

10,, Karen Reivich and Andrew Shatté, *The Resilience Factor: 7 Keys to Finding Your Inner Strength and Overcoming Life's Hurdles* (New York: Three Rivers Press, 2003), 9-30.

11 Reivich and Shatté, *The Resilience Factor: 7 Keys to Finding Your Inner Strength and Overcoming Life's Hurdles*, 25-47.

12 Andrew Zolli and Ann Marie Healy, *Resilience: Why Things Bounce Back* New York: Simon & Schuster, 2012,), 7.

of resiliency, "Accordingly, we frame resiliency... as the capacity of a system, enterprise, or a person to maintain its core purpose and integrity in the face of dramatically changed circumstances."[13] An insightful read, the authors reveal the steps to take to rebuild life, to reorganize in the throes of disaster, and to use unsettling events to spur new creativity, fresh solutions, and new paths on the road to wholeness, wellness, or organizational success. They provide wisdom for the ages in unveiling both their resilience imperative and the importance of dealing with the volatile winds of change, albeit storm winds of change. They say, "If we cannot control the tides of change, we can learn to build better boats."[14]

I think of Noah facing his critics, rain (for the first time), a flood, and building a boat. I think of Moses leading God's people through the wilderness, and his capacity for adapting to lead through drought, scarce food, and a quest for water. I think of King David running for his life, hiding in caves, surviving betrayal at the hands of his son Absalom, and walking through sin and grief. I think of the resilient apostle Paul, determined yet often

---

13 Zolli and Healy, *Resilience: Why Things Bounce Back*, 7.
14 Zolli and Healy, *Resilience: Why Things Bounce Back*, 5.

deterred, graceful yet often disgraced, and hopeful even in hopeless situations. I think of faith in God and Christ by the power of the Holy Spirit as the resilience factor and imperative.

Still, two more things must be said as I am on the way to tell you why I am writing this book. Researchers over the last ten to twelve years have discussed the strength of the resilient (bouncing back), the power of the robust (holding your own, which is sometimes the best you can do), and the muscle of the antifragile. How do things progress after trauma, in spite of adversity, and move beyond the robust and resilient and fragile to make progress?[15]

The resilient bounce back. The robust hold their ground. Most things are fragile, breakable, and subject to brokenness like a mason jar, a table, or even a house when the roof leaks. Life spins in much more complex patterns, is fragile yes, but antifragile, that is, gives a person the ability to grow, mature, and renew itself through difficult circumstances. The fragile aim to control, to predict life, even worry and over-calculate events in realms of speculation. In other words, the fragile

---

15 Nassim Nicholas Taleb, *Antifragile: Things that Gain from Disorder* (New York: Random House, 2014), 5.

worry themselves about what might or might not happen, worry themselves to death, so to speak.

Nassim Taleb says, "Wind extinguishes a candle and energizes a fire."[16] He calls for growth, thriving in the stress, trauma, and troubles of life while declaring the antifragile as "anything that has more upside than downside to random events (or certain shocks)."[17] He encourages and concludes: grow through the trauma, learn from your mistakes, do not avoid risk, adapt, and enjoy times of volatility, and "the best way to verify if you are alive is by checking if you like variations."[18] Change happens. Trauma comes. Stress builds. Tragedy shocks. Disappointment deadens the soul. More than only the strong survive, the antifragile finds ways to thrive amid thorns, valleys, and dark times.

Now I walked you down this path to tell you what happened. I started to write a book on resiliency. My friend, Rockbridge Seminary President Daryl Eldridge called. "We are helping our seminary students understand the importance of resiliency. "Write something on that," I recall him

---

16 Taleb, *Antifragile: Things that Gain from Disorder*, 3.

17 Taleb, *Antifragile: Things that Gain from Disorder*, 5.

18 Taleb, *Antifragile: Things that Gain from Disorder*, 423.

saying as we talked. Then, an hour later, a friend who serves as a military chaplain phoned. "What are you focusing on in spiritual development?" I quizzed. "We are working hard to teach these men and women who serve our country as soldiers the importance of resiliency, personally, in the military, and, of course, spiritually."

Not long after that, my friend Taylor and I discussed the concepts of resiliency, robustness, and the antifragile. Books were suggested along the way. Insights were added. Wisdom was spun in words. I concluded that in life we are sometimes resilient (bounce back!), sometimes robust (hold your own! You can do it!), and antifragile (the wind blows where it will, blows out some candles, fans the flames of fire to energize others... we have an upside in the downside of life!). I concluded, after reading 2 Timothy 2:1, "You then, my son, be strong in the grace that is in Christ Jesus."

I write to help you (and me) be strong in God's grace. I write to assist each of us in bouncing back, holding our own, and working toward the upside of grace in the downside of life. I write to help both of us look upward when life pulls downward, pushes backward, and impedes our movement forward. I write to benefit the heart, mind, and soul in the adventure of grace that finds strength by faith in Christ in the marvelous adventure called life. I write to acknowledge the reality of trouble, trauma, stress, detours, disappointments, and dead ends in our lives. I write to find grace under the shadow of God's wings.

I write to answer these dilemmas: How do people recover to find purposeful lives? How do they face the paralyzing forces of fear and move forward with renewed energy? How do people resurrect life's meaning after the despair of failure? How do people power through the valleys to climb new vistas of faith to find fruit in their labors?

Be strong in the grace. In this book we will discuss the sacred. We will talk about sacred grit. How can you push through events in life when you feel like giving up? How can sad, even sorrowful, even shocking events pull us toward the sacred? The first chapter will discuss sacred fear, moving from fear to courage. A soldier will instruct us. The second chapter will discuss sacred agony, transforming failure into success. An athlete will inspire us. The third chapter will discuss sacred sweat, labor as a key to move toward faith to fruitfulness. A farmer and his grit will guide us.

If you look up sacred in Latin, the gamut runs wild from *sacra* or *sacer* (sacred) to *sacerdotalis* (priestly) to *sacramentum* (an oath and guarantee or deposit of money in a lawsuit) to *sacrarium* (shrine, chapel, sacred place) to *sacrificium* (sacrifice) to *sacrilegium* (sacrilege; temple robbing, violation of sacred rites). What is sacred requires value, a pledge or oath to its value, and a sacrificial element, holding nothing back if you will, giving your all to it, as if your life depended on it. To violate or to demonstrate violence toward the sacred proves sacrilegious, a kind of temple robbing, and definite violation of sacred rites.

In antiquity, the Roman concept of *sacra* combined two ideas: first, in a religious sense of homage to a god or family sacred rites, an oath or pledge, especially in honor of burial for a relative; two, in a legal sense, *sacra* later connected to Roman law in legal inheritance, legal rights passed from one generation to the next. In a religious sense in antiquity, Romans pledged to their god or deity by giving up something or removing something from their presence, like a bull, piece of bread, cake or wine. The sacrifice ("to make sacred") was then made to the god on the altar by sacrificing the bull, leaving the bread at the altar, placing the cake on the altar, or pouring the wine over the altar. A religious act involved a sacred act.

If you look up the word "grit" in a dictionary, you will find it formed meaning in its Old English and Scottish ancestry. To the English, grit formed particles like sand or gravel, the kind of stuff you might wash off the window or off your face after a sandstorm. To the English, grit meant a firmness of character, determination, and strength, like a man or woman gritting his or her teeth and pressing forward in a strong wind, life storm, or horrific event. Those who grit, clench their teeth and jaws, and endure the agony with grace. The Scottish used grit as an adjective, understanding those with "grit" were indeed "great." Grittiness inspired greatness of character, activity, or resolve in the worst of times. Only the grit of the great inspired others to greatness as well as portrayed a model to imitate grittiness.

I welcome you to sacred grit. I invite you into the sacred, to walk through the door of a sacred journey, and discover how fear, failure, and faith invite us into a journey with the sacred acts of God to grow toward Christlikeness and mature us in

His image. I bid you join me as we explore sacred grit in the shadow of God's grace. Turn the page and walk softly, tiptoe, and listen for the voice that speaks.

Sacred Fear

From Fear to Courage

"There will come a time when you believe everything is finished; that will be the beginning."

~ Louis L'Amour, *Lonely on the Mountain*[19]

"IT'S NUMBER NINETEEN," THE dentist remarked while she smiled.

A large window set the scene for a wonderful fall day. Leaves wafted in the wind and fell off

---

19 Louis L'Amour, *Lonely on the Mountain*

trees. Sunlight cascaded down from the heavens. Dew tickled the morning grass. It's number nineteen.

When Juan Gonzalez played outfield for baseball's Texas Rangers, he smashed homeruns and wore jersey number nineteen. Clint Longley wore number nineteen, punched number twelve Roger Staubach in the mouth at an NFL Football training camp one year, and led the Dallas Cowboys to a remarkable Thanksgiving Day victory over the Washington Redskins years later. Shooting Guard Tony Campbell wore nineteen for basketball's Dallas Mavericks back in the nineties. It was one of the few times any player ever wore nineteen for the Mavericks. Former Dallas Maverick coach, Don Nelson, wore number nineteen when he played for the Boston Celtics. Willis Reed played for the New York Knicks in the NBA, and went to the basketball Hall Of Fame wearing number nineteen on his jersey.

My favorite numbered jerseys, by the way, hail as twelve (Roger Staubach, Dallas Cowboys NFL football), forty-one (Dirk Nowitzki, Dallas Mavericks NBA basketball), ten (Jim Sundberg, Texas Rangers MLB baseball), twenty-three (Michael Jordan (Chicago Bulls, NBA basketball), and

seven. Seven is the perfect number. Nineteen, at least for me, turned out to be bad luck.

"See? It's number nineteen," rolled through my brain as I glanced back and forth, through the window at the dentist and at the x-ray on the computer screen. My tooth had broken, number nineteen. Who counts teeth? Who numbers them? Who breaks them?

One night at dinner I felt a rock, or a large piece of gravel, in the roast chewed in my mouth. The rock was my tooth. One day earlier I ate Pecan Pie and felt something strange, movement on my left jaw, and a bizarre feeling in the mouth. Number nineteen, apparently, had been preparing to act like a rock in my meat, and it happened.

The dentist, kind and compassionate, sent me to an oral surgeon. D-day came, the day I had long dreaded. Rain pelted the earth on the outside. Office music, oral surgeon music, played majestic and melodious tunes in the waiting room. I waited. Number nineteen, or what was left of it, was about to come out. Such sweet, soft music usually preludes the blast of a drill, dissonance, and the loud crash in the musical score.

A door opened. A nice lady wearing the uniform called my name. I got up, walked through the door, and took my seat in the reclining chair. The music stopped.

The uniformed lady prepared the equipment. The oral surgeon entered the door wearing a white coat. He explained the procedure and reinforced the task of retrieving number nineteen.

He placed blue rubber gloves on his hands. He reached for, and found, a silver syringe with a REALLY long needle. He stung me three or four times, began his work, talked to his assistant in oral surgeon code language, and began to drill, so it seemed. I know the crack of a bat in baseball, the clash of a helmet in football, and the squeak of a shoe in basketball as it rubs the court. A new sound emerged.

My right jaw had a rubber block in it to keep my mouth open, and to keep me from biting my invader. My eyes noted everything, silver utensils, gauze, stiches, and tooth tweezers, if that is what you call the tweezer-like utensil lowered into my mouth.

The oral surgeon did a wonderful job working like an experienced mechanic lowering his head into the engine to work on the car. Then he mumbled words I shall never forget, "You will hear a crackling sound. Your tooth is brittle." The

cracking sound crackling, I wish to inform you, signaled to my nerves, my brain in high function, and my heart pumping faster, the sound of my tooth, piece by piece being mined like spark plugs in an engine, one piece at a time, or being mined like quartz rocks from the side of a mountain. My tooth cracked, and in just minutes the oral surgeon extracted tooth number nineteen.

He and his assistant sent me home with pain medication prescriptions ("Take this!"), bloody gauze in my mouth ("Your jaw might swell a bit, but this will only hurt for a few days!"), and good wishes for the coming days of jaw popping and mouth-numbing joy ("You should be fine, but if not give us a call!").

For some reason, before the oral surgery procedure, my heart raced, my palms began to sweat, my arm pits felt wet and sticky, and my blood pressure rose more than slightly. "Your blood pressure is up," the assistant said.

"Yes," I replied. "The whole thought of the dentist office, oral surgery, and shiny, silver utensils on my teeth makes me nervous. I know the women who have had babies, endured great pain, and they come in here tough and ready to tackle the pain. Men like me come in here crying.

They can play football and stuff, but the thought of pain makes grown men cry."

"White coat syndrome," she said. "We see it all the time." She laughed at my "women are tough, men are babies" comment. She thought what I had said was funny. Human nature often masks fear with humor. Extracting number nineteen, the oral surgeon, and the thought of crackling teeth, stitches in my mouth, and blood in my mouth raised my fear quotient.

Fear features as one of the most emotional responses in the human anatomy. Fear answers as one of the most human of responses in human history. Fear's responders in the nerves, neural transmitters, and brain function barrage the heart, mind, and soul with multiple messages that confuse and confound the body once at ease.

Fear operates in the human anatomy and in human history in various ways. A child may be fearless on a zip-line, or swimming in an ocean, or catching tadpoles at the pond, yet may feel terrified at the sight of a strange black bird close at hand, a jellyfish in the ocean water, or a pinching crab in the sand by his or her foot. A woman may sit down on an airplane as relaxed as a bird in a nest, yet see a spider with an orange dot on her

dress and scream bloody murder. An NFL football player may feel comfortable in his skin and wreak havoc on an opposing quarterback on Sunday in front of ninety-thousand people, yet jump out of his skin at the sight of a grass snake on the back porch at his house. A hunter may love guns, yet be scared at his or her wit's end when a gun points in his or her direction. A person may adore his or her dog, yet run for his or her life in fear when a huge, barking, brown and white St. Bernard dog comes at you with white, snarling teeth. This happened to me once on a trip to a fishing pond, and while the dog did no harm, my antenna raise, my blood pressure rises, and my heart rate rises when large dogs approach.

"Don't be afraid of the dog," a man once said as his pit bull barked, almost tore the tree down, and tried to tear the chain off his neck to charge me. The chain had worn the tree at its bottom, and fear had wearied my racing heart. I made it past the dog to the door and told the dog owner, "I don't mean to be afraid. It just happens."

As a side note, the anatomy and your history work in sync in a moment like that. Your human anatomy, the brain, remembers the childhood dog incident from your past history. The result incites fear. Yes, oh yes, fear happens! You can name fear. Acrophobia notes a fear of heights. The claustrophobic person fears cramped, tight spaces like a closet. Agoraphobia includes the fear of open spaces or crowds. Arachnophobia is the fear of spiders. The person with cynophobia fears dogs or, worse yet, rabies. Felinophobia means the fear of cats. Hemophobia designates the fear of blood. Xenophobia is the fear of strangers. Acousticophobia indicates a fear of noise. Prosophobia defines the fear of progress. Aviophobia means a fear of flying. Latrophobia defines the fear of going to the doctor. Entomophobia labels as the fear of insects, creepy, crawly critters. Ecclesiophobia points to the fear of church. Cometophobia is the fear of comets. Liliophobia is the fear of speaking, and public speaking translates as one of most people's greatest fears. Hagiophobia specifies the fear of holy things, a fear of the sacred.

I have known people to fear heights, water, church, crowds, flying on an airplane, spiders, public speaking, snakes, and surgery. I have never known anyone who feared comets, cats, or cowbells. I have known people who refuse the sacred,

fear the sacred, and reject all things named holy or sacred. I have known people for whom fear caused paralysis, physically and emotionally, where they could not move forward because of indecisiveness or progress due to some tick in the mind that caused them to freeze in a given moment.

If you serve as a soldier you will discover that training and rigorous discipline help the soldier overcome fear, indecisiveness, and paralysis that lead to frozen moments at critical times. As a Christian, the apostle Paul instructs, "Be strong in God's grace." He further instructs, "Endure hardship with us like a good soldier of Christ Jesus" (2 Tim 2:3-4, NIV).

Often the idea of enduring hardness involves encountering, engaging, and enduring a difficult circumstance in life. It concentrates on pushing through the circumstance when you feel like giving in to it. It anticipates struggle, and even a strategy to push through. It endures in spite of the fact that a person wishes to engineer an escape. Enduring a difficulty, the pain of it, and the despair of it almost never gives pause for enjoyment. What endurance requires in hardship, though, might produce a sense of joy in the end: sacred grit that inspires the dedication and decisiveness of a soldier.

Paul writes to Timothy as a servant of Christ. "Timothy the timid," one might call him. Do not be critical of Timothy. Timidity, fear, and the paralysis of fear might arise from inexperience (the desire to do good), perfectionism (the desire to be perfect in the good), or simple fear (the instinctive desire to preserve the good self and survive). Most of you reading this book have experienced fear in some form. I know I have: in the oral surgeon's chair, at night when sounds go bump in the night, and when I sat before my examiners at the conclusion of my Ph. D. in Cambridge, England. On that day, my palms began to sweat, my arm pits perspired, and my heart raced. Calm came, though, and calm prevailed so that I pushed through and delivered the news my examiners aimed to mine. That day, for lack of a better term, was like pulling teeth.

Life catches us in between, often at extremes: between the comfortable oral surgeon's chair versus the uncomfortable tooth extraction; between the determination-decisiveness of a soldier at war versus the thought of quitting and the paralysis of some circumstance we might describe as a real battle; between courage as the overcoming of fear and fear itself.

Franklin D. Roosevelt once spoke as President of the United States on the edge of a precipice and WWII, stating, "The only thing we have to fear is fear itself." A nice quote FDR, but when itself becomes yourself, and fear becomes personal, real, emotional, even uncontrollable, fearing fear might seem your only option. People do fear fear itself.

C. K. Chesterton responded to a remark about Robert L. Stevenson's comments in a letter about his childhood fear of the beasts with many eyes in the *Book of Revelation*. He replied, "I like those monsters beneath the throne very much. But I like them beneath the throne."[20] I guess a common childhood fear might be the dentist, or a dog, or monsters with big eyes that you like to stay out of sight under the throne, or at least under the bed with their big eyes so that your scared bug eyes do not have to see them.

I can think of three times I feared fear itself and felt afraid. First, in elementary school I arrived home after a movie. The popcorn and

---

20 Kevin Belmonte, *The Quotable Chesterton* (Nashville: Thomas Nelson, 2011), 175.

coke allowed the consumption of nervous energy in the fright night flick that incited fear. I cannot tell you too much about the movie except the title: *The Legend of Boggy Creek.* The movie distilled fear by showing scene after scene of the legend, an ape-like, gorilla-like monster that flashed in front of people in a car on a dark road; that devoured squealing pigs from a pig farmer's barns in the middle of the night; and one scene where a man sat on the toilet when the monster lunged at him through a door that burst open suddenly. The scenes portrayed an entire community's fear, vivid scenes depicting the monster on the loose that could show up on your doorstep, burst through your bathroom door, or devour you like popcorn any minute.

    To this day the pictorial elements of the film stick in my mind. Arriving home, the headlamps on the car shone in the tree in our driveway and on the white garage door. For some unknown reason, all the house lights were turned off, both inside and out. The way the house was positioned, the headlamps from the car offered no help as I ran in fear under the huge oak tree by the sidewalk and beat on the front door. It was as if the monster was on the rampage, coming after me. Relief came as the door opened, lights went on, and the click of the lock once inside protected me from the legend on the loose.

Second, I felt an intense fear one night in the mountains of North Carolina at my grandmother's house in the mountains. An adult with children, I had traveled to see my two aunts who lived in the house. In the pitch blackness of a mountain night, I heard a squeaking of the bed upstairs, the rustling of feet, the whispering voices of my two aunts, and the sound of a car moving on the gravel just above the house on the side of the road.

"Do you see it? Did you see the car lights go off? Is anybody walking in the yard? I think I see someone," the whispering voices volleyed back and forth in conversation. I either saw a person in the shadows on the porch in front of the window across the room from my bed or imagined it. I never said a word to my aunts who often lived in fear. But I remained still, hearing every sound: crickets chirping, creaks in the house, cicadas whining and singing, curtains ruffled by the wind in an open window, and two old ladies crawling back into bed in the room above. Minutes later a car started, the gravel groused, headlamps lit the road, and a car moved onto the road and disappeared in the fog.

Fear heightened my senses and alerted the soldier's mechanism of defense and self-preservation. I prepared to fight, sat still in the bed, waited, and fell asleep after the car disappeared.

Third, I felt a sense of fear when my mother had a heart attack and slept several days in the hospital in ICU. The doctor did not offer glowing reports. Waiting proved the hardest part. Endurance, both hers and mine, proved intense, exhausting. Fear ignited fires of worry. Worry spread like a grass fire to make me wonder about the future. The uncertain future produced unwarranted fears about a life without mother. Fear subsided when miraculously she pulled through to laugh again, and live again.

Fear can cause us to run, or run scared like imaginary monsters chasing us. Fear can paralyze us like noises that arrest the senses in the night. Fear can attack us and make us worry about the future. Multiple fears add up to internal pressure. A volcano of fear builds inside the heart, mind, and soul. Pressure builds. Sacred grit transforms sacred pressure into a prize for future days.

No one faces pressure, faces fear, faces the unknown better than a soldier.

When Paul wrote to Timothy, soldiers stood, marched, fought, and watched as a common feature of the Roman world. Soldiers fought in bloody battles. Soldiers protected garrisons, gates, and borders in intimidating Roman style. Soldiers patrolled streets, neighborhoods, forums, and the *agora* or marketplace like today's open air market or Wal-Mart where people purchase food for dinner.

If you read the New Testament, soldiers rolled dice beneath the cross of Christ, quelled uprisings, bound and guarded prisoners with chains, and interacted up close and personal with the apostle Paul. The apostle must have soldier episodes in his mind. Consider this account from Acts:

"Then he called two of his centurions and ordered them, 'Get ready a detachment of two hundred soldiers, seventy horsemen and two hundred spearmen to go to Caesarea at nine tonight. Provide mounts for Paul so that he may be taken safely to Governor Felix.'
He wrote a letter as follows:
Claudius Lysias,
To His Excellency, Governor Felix:

Greetings.

This man was seized by the Jews and they were about to kill him, but I came with my troops and rescued him, for I had learned that he is a Roman citizen. I wanted to know why they were accusing him, so I brought him to their Sanhedrin. I found that the accusation had to do with questions about their law, but there was no charge against him that deserved death or imprisonment. When I was informed of a plot to be carried out against the man, I sent him to you at once. I also ordered his accusers to present to you their case against him. So the soldiers, carrying out their orders, took Paul with them during the night and brought him as far as Antipatris. The next day they let the cavalry go on with him, while they returned to the barracks. When the cavalry arrived in Caesarea, they delivered the letter to the governor and handed Paul over to him. The governor read the letter and asked what province he was from. Learning that he was from Cilicia, he said, 'I will hear your case when your accusers get here.' Then he ordered that Paul be kept under guard in Herod's palace" (Acts 23:23-35, NIV).

The letter indicates that Roman law was at work. Should Paul be punished, kept under lock and key, or set free? The letter shows the prominent, up close and personal acts of soldiers under Paul's nose. A Roman soldier held honor, took risks, endured hardship, encountered suffering, and dedicated himself to the power, glory, and honor of the Roman Empire.

"Soldier" in Greek translates as *stratiotes*, a "strategist" in training, protection, and war. In truth, the Roman concept of a soldier and its reality found itself connected to Greco-Roman philosophy, Roman power, and Roman ideals. A soldier in terms of Greco-Roman philosophy aimed to the "good." This means more than being a good boy or good girl or a mother saying to her child, "I will give you candy if you are good."

Greek philosophy hailed the good man as one who pledged allegiance to government authority, who fulfilled duties and obligations based on the law, and who obeyed at the command of a superior.

The Roman orator, statesman, politician, and lawyer (102-43 B.C.) named Cicero, in his book *On Duties*, acknowledged four virtues: wisdom, justice, fortitude, and self-control. An emperor, a citizen, and a solider no less, each held honor toward the virtues and sought to achieve them in the wider kingdom, their families, and their personal lives. Soldiers dressed in their garb: tunics, stringed sandals, helmets, breastplates, spears, and shields. They held posts from which they would not depart. They took commands (do this!) and even prohibitions (don't do this!), which they always fulfilled as obligations. They pledged an oath of allegiance, which they never disregarded at any moment.

The Roman soldier is depicted visually in our modern day; on the arch of Titus on the Appian way in Rome; on ancient relics of architecture carved on marble stone in Rome's decayed pillars and buildings; in the frescoes and art work saved by the British Museum in London or the Metropolitan museum in New York; and in film and movies, like Easter movies about Jesus and the cross with a soldier dressed in grab carrying a sword and shield while laughing and rolling dice for Jesus's purple robe, or an old movie with the chariot racing Ben Hur displaying Roman dedication.

If I could coin one word for the Greco-Roman soldier in the sense of virtue, in the sense of a good

man, in the sense of the good soldier, it would be dedication. A Roman soldier served as a totally dedicated soldier.

The Roman soldier also took risks, fought with force and will, resolved to win. Roman soldiers, after military victories, marched into Rome in a festive procession, behind the emperor, while carrying the spoils of war as people gathered, cheered, praised, and waved palm branches. If a Roman served in dedicated fashion in Greco-Roman glory, the display of Roman power by a soldier meant that the soldier went to great lengths of loyalty, bravery, and put himself at the risk of personal danger for the higher cause of the kingdom. A soldier held honor, but also appeared as a heroic, risk-taking, noble adventurer who sought to gain praise, glory, and honor from the emperor, his peers, and the general populace.

The Roman ideal of the Roman soldier involved the protection of Rome, the expansion of Roman borders, and the maintenance of law and order. Roman soldiers enforced, and oftentimes coerced Roman law. Roman soldiers quelled revolts, stopped rebellions and uprisings, and presented themselves as keeper of the law, and promoters, albeit with force, of *pax romana*, that is, Roman peace.

The Jewish historian, aristocrat, priest, and political leader Flavius Josephus (A.D. 37-100) spoke of the Roman soldier. He was born in Jerusalem then later exiled to Rome, but wrote of Jewish antiquities and wars. He writes: "no confusion breaks their customary formation, no panic paralyzes, no fatigue exhausts; ...duties (obligations) are performed with the same discipline, the same regard for security."[21] Josephus tells us much about the good soldier, one of good order who follows the good command, who possesses good fortitude, who is trained with good discipline so as not to neglect any duty.

Philosophically, the Stoic philosopher Epictetus (A.D. 55-135) asked, "Do you not know that the business of life is a campaign (*strateia*, strategy, military strategy like a soldier)?"[22] The former slave, freed to live and ponder life's deep meaning, viewed life as a kind of battle. In regard to Greco-Roman concepts, Roman power, and Roman ideals of peace, Epictetus saw the good and excellent in terms of two words: order and

---

21 Josephus, *Jewish War* 3.71-109.
22 Epictetus, *Discourses* 3.24.31.

obedience. In simple terms, he believed in *eutaktos*, good order through tactics, strategy and *eupeithos*, good response to the command given.[23]

Epictetus honored the good soldier and admonished the not-so-good soldier. He said, "But you neglect to perform the duties assigned to you by your commanding officer, and complain when some hard order is given you, and fail to understand to what state you are bringing the army, as far is on you lies; because if they imitate you, no one will dig a trench, no one will construct a palisade (fence or wall), or watch through the night, or risk his life in fighting, but they will seem useless soldiers."[24] Epictetus described a bad soldier, one not to imitate, one who neglects duty, one who complains about hardness.

It is no small wonder Paul wrote this to Timothy: endure hardness as a good soldier. It is no small wonder that Timothy knew and witnessed the Roman concepts, power, and ideals of the soldier. It is no small wonder that I have told you this because sacred grit demands that you serve as a good soldier of Jesus Christ.

---

23 Epictetus, *Discourses* 3.24.95.
24 Epictetus, *Discourses* 3.24.31-33.

A good soldier pledges allegiance to Christ, serves faithfully, honors duty, and risks the personal in honor of the more noble kingdom goals. A good soldier does not neglect duty, sets an example for others to follow and imitate. A good soldier rarely complains. I say rarely because God's grace gives us room for humanity and life, as a battle campaign often conjures up stuff over which to complain. Endure hardness as a good soldier.

What about hardness? Not long ago a country and western singer posted a picture of a man praying for an American soldier at an airport. Singer Sunny Sweeney's amazing soldier in prayer went viral and received thousands of "likes." She acknowledged having a bad day, saw the two men praying, and posted the picture with a caption: "I watched this whole thing go down in an airport and felt like sharing it with you." Sunny Sweeny, the girl whose songs *Bad Girl Phase* and *From a Table Away*, shed tears when she witnessed the good act and the prayer for the soldier. Good things still happen.

But imagine with me for a moment, the hardness of a soldier's life separated from family; uncertainty as certain as the fatigues he or she wears; in war; tired; dirty; hungry; at risk of

bombs, bullets, and blinding swift attacks; angry at times, lonely at times, hurting at times, despaired at times. I have never been a soldier, but once a soldier described life as a soldier that went something like this: "Boredom, then panic; anxiety, worry, then a rush of activity; trying to keep it together and after a battle trying to put everything and everyone back together." A broken cord requires tedious effort to mend.

The colloquial phrase, "Soldier on" applies to any soldier. Press on. Endure hardness.

As I write to you the reality of hardness hits home. Protests in Ferguson, Missouri draw attention to grief, anxiety, tension, and confusion. A family I know just lost their young college-age daughter in an automobile accident. Soldiers receive news that they are staying in Afghanistan longer than expected. Ice storms and snow storms pound the east coast, creating a sea of white, airport delays, and fear of electricity grids overloading and electrical power in homes being shut down for days as often happens. A single mother, who just had her car repaired, wakes up, drinks her morning coffee, struggles to pay her bills, dresses for the day, and enters her repaired car on which she spent half of her small fortune to repair, and the car does not start. Hardness arrives in big, overwhelming global news, or in everyday, small doses. Hardness can rob you of desire, the desire to press on, the desire to press on in adversity, or the desire to simply give up. Have you ever felt like giving up?

Hardness indicates a combination of bad, evil, and the suffering that goes with it. Hardness involves emotional, physical, and spiritual suffering. Hardness potentially confuses common sense, distances compassion toward others and the self, and internalizes suffering intensely. Hardness aims to refuse the sacred, marginalize the sacred, and destroy the sacred in your life.

But for you, good soldier, good news arrives like the announcement of a new baby. The good soldier finds strength in God's grace (2 Corinthians 12:9). The good soldier can endure. The good soldier can endure hardness. It might actually be the one thing God delivers to strengthen your faith or equip you for greater ministry. The hardness might serve as a way to softness, finding God's grace sufficient for the suffering at hand, finding his compassion in the difficulty, finding his strong hand to hold your weak hand, or might be an avenue down which you travel that you lend a hand to another down the road.

This kind of comment, pain for the present to comfort others in the future, is never the goal of hardness, much less hardship, but can supply inspiration, opportunity, or care for another individual because your pain sticks to your guts and your soul, and supplies Christ-like empathy for others if you allow it.

Note three words in the apostle Paul's thought—praise, comfort, and endurance: "Praise be to the God and Father of our Lord Jesus Christ, the Father of compassion and the God of all comfort, who comforts us in all our troubles, so that we can comfort those in any trouble with the comfort we ourselves have received from God. For just as the sufferings of Christ flow over into our lives, so also through Christ our comfort overflows. If we are distressed, it is for your comfort and salvation; if we are comforted, it is for your comfort, which produces in you patient endurance of the same sufferings we suffer. And our hope for you is firm, because we know that just as you share in our sufferings, so also you share in our comfort" (2 Corinthians 1:3-7, NIV).

Your first question should be, "What did Paul mean?" He meant that hardness and hardship move us to seek God's comfort, and that having received Divine comfort, we can comfort others as Christ comforted us. If, as it seems, we are clay in the Potter's hands, moldable, pliable, shapeable, and soft enough in spite of the hardness of circumstances, we are molded like clay to care and comfort others, after or in the midst of their pain.

Will you be clay in God's hands, or be rock-like, hard and inflexible? If you are clay, you allow God to be the Rock, acknowledging that He is already the Rock. If you act rock-like, you might miss the blessing of God's shaping hand, and the joy of extending a hand to comfort another. Simply put, life is no picnic and you cannot always control the pain, but you can find and dish out God's comfort.

Your second question might be, "Did Paul ever suffer hardship, endure hardness?" You better believe it! Reading Paul's journal of crises might make you think your hardness isn't all that bad. Paul stated his hardship as occasional and often painful hardness. Paul speaks in defense of himself, and, if I may say, quite defensively. Imagine that a friend has offended you or a co-worker has criticized you with harsh and hard words, or that your spouse has angered you with mean words. This happens to Paul and he responds:

"What anyone else dares to boast about—I am speaking as a fool—I also dare to boast about. Are they Hebrews? So am I. Are they Israelites? So am I. Are they Abraham's descendants? So am I. Are they servants of Christ? (I am out of my mind to talk like this.) I am more. I have worked much harder, been in prison more frequently, been flogged more severely, and been exposed to death again and again. Five times I received from the Jews the forty lashes minus one. Three times I was beaten with rods, once I was stoned, three times I was shipwrecked, I spent a night and a day in the open sea, I have been constantly on the move. I have been in danger from rivers, in danger from bandits, in danger from my own countrymen, in danger from Gentiles; in danger in the city, in danger in the country, in danger at sea; and in danger from false brothers. I have labored and toiled and have often gone without sleep; I have known hunger and thirst and have often gone without food; I have been cold and naked. Besides everything else, I face daily the pressure of my concern for all the churches. Who is weak, and I do not feel weak? Who is led into sin, and I do not inwardly burn? If I must boast, I will boast of the things that show my weakness. The God and Father of the Lord Jesus, who is to be praised forever, knows *that I am not lying. In Damascus the governor under King Aretas had the city of the Damascenes guarded in order to arrest me. But I was lowered in a basket from a window in the wall and slipped through his hands"* (2 Corinthians 11:21-33, NIV).

Did you see, feel, and identify with Paul's hardness list of hardship? From prison to pride as temptation, from poverty to poundings on his body, from danger to disaster, from weakness and worrisome realities, and from the threat of kings to the threat of death, and from the risk of near death in the high drama of a basket lowered by a rope so that he could escape in the heart-racing, blood-pressure rising, and foot-fleeing moment of fear's thrill.

By the way, I discover in Scripture, hardness is a common theme among the saints of God: Jacob wrestling with God at the fjord of the Jabbok River; Moses in the wilderness of Midian; David in fields, in caves, in battles, on the run, and facing a giant in Goliath; the prophet Jeremiah in a well or cistern praying to survive; and John exiled in darkness on the small Greek isle of Patmos on the beautifully blue Aegean Sea.

Jacob endured hardness and found the soft heart of God in liberation. David survived, even surviving his own son's betrayal while standing at the gates of Jerusalem and Absalom's death, to find suffering a reality and God's song (psalm) a comfort in the night. Jeremiah found a rope and hope to escape, and to proclaim the good news again, in spite of the bad news, cause for despair, and hardness as harshness all around.

John in exiled darkness found just enough of God's light to reveal the Revelation, and the truth that a little light in a dark place is really all you need, and that even in darkness you have potential to do your very best work in the eyes of God, especially if you open your eyes to God's vision. Read the revelation to see what I mean: visions amid divisions; hope in hopelessness; light in darkness; a grand future in the joy of a grand banquet in spite of the message of John's present day of an empty cupboard with no food or guests, like a house destroyed by a flood or a tornado.

Hardness might actually pave the road to better things (yes!), better days (can they get any worse?), and better hope for tomorrow (fear of no hope in the wilderness, facing the giant, in a dark time, or in exile moves to, yes, yes, oh yes, hope!).

"Endure hardness," Paul's words almost seem harsh, too hot to handle, too hard to handle, too much like a commanding officer shouting instruction to a soldier. Paul knew hardness. Paul experienced hardness. Paul felt hardness. More than likely Paul's knowledge, experience, feelings, and faith led him to supply Timothy with a Christian soldier's advice for him to place in his backpack for living the daily battle.

My own life looks nothing like Paul's list, but because hardness becomes personal, the hardness is nonetheless as real the apostle's Paul. My list could continue for pages, but your list is more important. What is your hardness list or your hardest hardness that aimed to harm your soul? I think back to sickness, sadness, grief, and glory unfulfilled, to disappointment with circumstances and other people, to a most common hardness, maybe the hardest hardness of all, disappointment with myself.

A complex hardness, might be, if you read Philip Yancey, *Disappointment with God*. Yet disappointment on all fronts, or any fronts in your life, does not have to stick to your soul like a smudge of grease on your white jeans. Disappointment can actually find cleansing in following

Paul's advice to Timothy as a precursor to his advice to endure hardness. What advice does Paul give?

Paul tells Timothy, "So do not be ashamed to testify about our Lord, or ashamed of me his prisoner. But join with me in suffering for the gospel, by the power of God, who has saved us and called us to a holy life—not because of anything we have done but because of his own purpose and grace" (2 Timothy 1:8-9, NIV). Partake of grace, partake of hardness (2 Timothy 1:8), Paul indicates, adding later that God's power, grace, mercy, and light supply the strength to endure.

Paul invites Timothy and the good soldier of Christ to join him in suffering, to partake of hardness as you partake of grace. Join the hardness, in a sense, to God's grace and the power of the Gospel. Join the hardness and rekindle God's fresh work in you (2 Timothy 1:6). Join hardness to God's grace, and overcome the spirit of timidity and fear (2 Timothy 1:9). Join hardness to God's grace, and treasure anew the power, love, and discipline of God's strength as a good soldier.

Sacred grit inspires sacred fear. You find afresh the meaning of God's power in fearing and trusting Him. "In God I trust; I will not be afraid.

What can man do to me? (Psalm 56:11, NIV). "The Lord is my light and my salvation—whom shall I fear? The Lord is the stronghold of my life—of whom shall I be afraid?" (Psalm 27:1, NIV). You discover anew God's love unfailing.

"Let those who fear the Lord say: 'His love endures forever.' In my anguish I cried to the Lord, and he answered by setting me free. The Lord is with me; I will not be afraid. What can man do to me? The Lord is with me; he is my helper. I will look in triumph on my enemies" (Psalm 118:4-7, NIV).

You discern God's grace sufficient and learn to love him, wait on him, rest in him, anchor your life in his goodness, and take courage to endure. "I am still confident of this: I will see the goodness of the Lord in the land of the living. Wait for the Lord; be strong and take heart and wait for the Lord" (Psalm 27:13-14, NIV).

Sacred grit, Paul shares, moves us toward the sacred, toward holiness despite the hardness (God saved us and called us to a "holy"...sacred... calling, 2 Timothy 1:9), and toward sacred fear to fear God and trust God in your dire circumstances. To be strong and to take heart involves

demonstrating sacred grit, a sacred fear of God that leads to courage, and a courage that overcomes fear.

Years ago I sat in the church parking lot of a church I once pastored. One cold, icy February day when a north wind blew, pain and fear swept over my heart like winds from a storm. Pain had caused a kind of indecisive paralysis in my leadership. I was stuck like a car in the mud. Fear had caused a deep darkness, yearning for light, begging for a glimpse of light. I was stuck, and in the darkness no way out seemed possible.

The church was in decline. The grimness of the weather mirrored my grim heart. I was failing in all that I had given my heart to. Like Jacob at the Jabbok River I wrestled with God. Like David I hid in a cave, and listened as my critics wagged their tongues in dismay at my leadership. Like Jeremiah in a cistern I longed for a rope to pull me out. Like John exiled on the isle of Patmos I called to the holiness of God for a vision, an answer, and a glorious message painted in colors like a rainbow in the sky. Like Paul, my heart, mind, soul, and career for that matter, seemed headed for a collision, a shipwreck on shores of destruction in the tossing waves of despair.

I would like to tell you that I heard angel voices, felt the touch on my hand of a golden rope, found gold at the end of the rainbow, and saw visions more grand than John's vision of Gog and Magog, and glassy seas, and the New Jerusalem descending from heaven. I would like to tell you that I was shocked to hear instruction from God's joyous, audible voice as a haven, and that God sent his golden chariots and legions of angels to call me, comfort me, console me, and coddle me like an eagle protecting her young in the nest. But, like the famed and infamous orator, the preacher, and the occasionally depressed saint Charles Haddon Spurgeon (1834-1892) penned from London, "There is no riding to heaven in a chariot; the rough way must be trodden; the mountains must be climbed, rivers must be forded, dragons must be fought, giants must be slain, difficulties must be overcome, and great trial must be born."[25] There is no riding to heaven in a chariot any more than there is an easy ride in a chariot here on earth.

No angelic voices came, and no visions thawed my icy, frost-filled, soul-chilled, paralyzed mind and my cold heart frozen in fear. I called out to

---

25 Steve Miller, ed., *C. H. Spurgeon on Spiritual Leadership* (Chicago: Moody Press, 2003), 124.

God, cried out in fear, cried real tears of despair, and carried on doing what God had called me to do, and learned to trust him. Rather than comfort, God kicked me in the seat of the pants and said, "Be strong in the grace." Rather than console, God arrested my senses and challenged me to be a good soldier in Christ Jesus. Rather than coddle me, God strengthened me, and shouted in hushed tones, "Be of good courage; I have overcome the world. Take heart. Fear not. Fret not. Do not be afraid!"

"Do not be afraid," bursts forth as God's common and core message to saints in the paralysis and indecisiveness of fear. "Do not be afraid," blasts away fear and moves us toward courage to follow, serve, and experience an adventure of faith carried by the wind of God's grace. "Do not be afraid," delivers a message to saints and sinners, souls in caves, on the run, in muddy places stuck, and in times when you need a rope to save your hide. "Do not be afraid," comes as a dispatch to saints and soldiers alike, fighting imaginary and real giants in the slingshot stretches and stones of hardness.

Jesus' disciples saw a ghost in the middle of the night on the Sea of Galilee. The weary, storm-tossed, fretful, and fearful disciples screamed. "A ghost! A *phantasm* (Greek)! A fantasy (Greek transliterated)!" Listen to Matthew write about the disciples afraid:

"But Jesus immediately said to them: 'Take courage! It is I. Don't be afraid.' 'Lord, if it's you," Peter replied,' tell me to come to you on the water.'
'Come,' he said.
Then Peter got down out of the boat, walked on the water and came toward Jesus. But when he saw the wind, he was afraid and, beginning to sink, cried out, 'Lord, save me!' Immediately Jesus reached out his hand and caught him. 'You of little faith,' he said, 'why did you doubt?' And when they climbed into the boat, the wind died down. Then those who were in the boat worshiped him, saying, 'Truly you are the Son of God'" (Matthew 14:27-33, NIV).

All of us are caught at times between fear and courage, doubt and faith, the rage of the storm and the calm of the storm, between fearing the storm and fearing God in the storm.

What did I do in my dark time of fear? I soldiered on. I pressed on. I kept doing what I knew to do by God's grace until he showed me something different. I swam my seas of difficulty, stayed in the water, in the battle, and trusted God, and the joy was all God's and all mine. I stayed and endured, and found joy in God's holiness by sacred fear that produced sacred grit that supplied a sacred blessing beyond my wildest dreams. Or maybe sacred grit imbued me with a sacred fear to take courage. I am not sure. Did you see that I "swam my sea of difficulty?" I developed a Hawaiian turtle shell.

Not long ago, I set sail on a sailboat and snorkeled off the coast of Maui, Hawaii, in the blue waters at the Molokini Crater. The crater juts out of the water, forming a moon-shaped, crescent-shaped island. The spot functions as a fabulous spot to snorkel, to view colorful fish, and even experience the thrill of danger. One person saw a baby shark inside the crater. If you move outside the crater, violent currents can carry you away never to be seen again. According to our tour guide, this happened once. "Adios. Goodbye you will be. Turn out the lights," he said or something like that as he explained to stay inside the crater.

Yellow-striped, purple-striped, and a rainbow array of colorful fish flashed and

sparkled beneath the waters inside the crater. Never have I viewed God's grandeur and wonder beneath the ocean's surface like that day.

Later in the tour, our guide took us to another prime spot to snorkel. "We're going to see sea turtles. They are large and some are over one hundred years old. Do not touch them. Their shells are really soft. If you touch these turtles you could receive up to a ten thousand dollar fine!" Ten-thousand was exaggerated. I later Googled and found the sea turtles were protected by law because they were endangered, lived to be over a hundred years old, scavenged for food like algae and kelp, and that you could receive a minimum of a five-hundred dollar fine for touching these beautiful and endangered species. In ancient days, sages forbid women on the isle of Maui to eat the Honu, the green turtle or tortoise, under threat of death. Generally, the honu do not threaten your safety, do not bite, and they survive and thrive in the blue waters below.

Of course, one man, acting like a child, did touch one the turtles like a child playing with forbidden fire on the stovetop. After announcing his touch, the tour guide again warned the swimmers and snorkelers, "Do not touch! Fines are possible!"

The green sea turtle possesses a shell, a carapace, green with light brown sections, that allow it to camouflage and protect itself in the depths of the sea. The carapace protects the turtle's body with a hard, outer shell that, if touched, feels like felt or soft, on the outside. If you touch the green sea turtle's shell, you might actually cause damage to the turtle.

My snorkeling expedition led to new discoveries: a sea turtle who soldiers on, survives and thrives by doing only what it knows to do, and what God made it to do, swim and scavenge, and has both a hard shell and a soft shell at the same time.

Thirty five years after my church parking lot fear and despair, and less than a year after my swimming expedition near the Molokini Crater in Maui, I have learned that a hard shell and a soft shell, like the turtle's, proves necessary on the expedition of faith. I endure hardness and form a hard shell, in a sense, committed to God's purpose, power, grace, mercy, and light no matter how rough the waters or the dangers. Like an exoskeleton that protects the honu and supplies structure and strength to keep it afloat, God's purpose, power, grace, mercy, and light form strength and structure of my life to keep me afloat by grace and faith. Like the soft part of the turtle's shell, God's purpose, power, grace, mercy, and light help me remain sensitive to touch, God's touch, other's touch, other's need for care and touch, and even aware of the touch of danger that lurks in rough waters, bizarre currents, and beyond the rim of the crater.

"Endure hardness" produces softness: dedicated like a soldier to God's cause, supplied with strength to face the hardness and harshness of the world's and personal troubles; and a hardness that softens the heart so that in humility you learn to trust God, and in service you aim to care with Christ-like compassion for people. God's grace hardens the shell for survival in life's rough waters, but God's grace softens the shell to help you celebrate, appreciate, and elevate God's goodness in the journey of joy.

You move from fear to courage in God's strength and by his grace. Be strong in the grace. Endue hardness as a good soldier. Be a good soldier of Jesus Christ. Do not touch sea turtles. And do not be afraid.

The good soldier allows God's good things to run wild in his or her heart, soul, and mind. G. K.

Chesterton said as simply as a sea turtle floating in water, "And the more I considered Christianity, the more I found that while it established a rule and order, the chief aim of that order was to give room for the good things to run wild."[26]

The good soldier can feel pain like a broken tooth, recognize there is no riding to heaven in a chariot, know that life swells with rough seas, and yet solider on in hope. After all, Jeremiah lamented, yet soldiered on in the hope of joy and the joy of hope and the fresh mercies of God new every morning like dew:

"He has broken my teeth with gravel; he has trampled me in the dust. I have been deprived of peace; I have forgotten what prosperity is. So I say, 'My splendor is gone and all that I had hoped from the Lord.' I remember my affliction and my wandering, the bitterness and the gall. I well remember them, and my soul is downcast within me. Yet this I call to mind and therefore I have hope: Because of the Lord's great love we are not consumed, for his compassions never fail. They are new every morning; great is your faithfulness. I say to myself, 'The

---

26 G. K. Chesterton, *Orthodoxy* Colorado Springs, Waterbook Press, 2001), 140-41.

Lord is my portion; therefore I will wait for him.' The Lord is good to those whose hope is in him, to the one who seeks him; it is good to wait quietly for the salvation of the Lord" (Lamentations 3:16-26, NIV).

Maybe Jeremiah once sat in a comfortable chair in an uncomfortable time when his tooth, broken like gravel in his mouth, when his fear arose, when affliction and pain bore down on his life in the dust of despair and the fear of hopelessness. Yet Jeremiah found the grace, the goodness of God in the courage of the good soldier, and the grace of God's compassion that no more fail than an oral surgeon plunging the depths to extract number nineteen. Be strong in the grace. You can do it!

Notes to the Reader

Oh reader, did you like my story about the oral surgeon? Did you wince when you read it? Do you want to know if I winced when I wrote it? I wanted you to know that everyday circumstances can create fear. I later told the oral surgeon and dentist, "It's not like I try to raise my blood

pressure and fear on purpose. For some unknown reason, it just happens."

You already know this I am sure, but psychologist will tell you and me that most fear roots in our childhood. Honestly, I am not afraid of much. But I will tell you the fear of dentists and oral surgeons root in my childhood. I wore braces for seven years, and every trip to the dentist required excruciating pain. I wore the old fashioned head gear at night to help move my teeth, and low and behold pain became my constant companion, my enemy, and my friend of betrayal. My brain signals my nerves, which recall my childhood memories, which then signals and shouts, "Brace yourself. The pain is coming. Blood pressure, rise! Heart, race! Palms, sweat! Attention, needles on deck. Prepare to meet thy doom!"

Of course, what my brain and nerves do at the dentist was exaggerated, but something like that happens when I feel discomfort in the comfortable dentist chair. Childhood fears often signal adult fears. Is my fear of snakes a result of lifting the dog house as a child and seeing the black snake coiled? Is it a result of my mother seeing the snake from the kitchen window and running with a hoe to chop that baby to smithereens? Is my occasional fear of dogs related to the barking St. Bernard on my fishing expedition? Is the fear I experienced when my mother had a heart attack in the hospital related to the day as a five year old that my mother and I were in a bad car wreck when God's fortune smiled and we survived. She survived in a hospital, a broken hip and a broken heart, and gratitude to God for survival in all the brokenness. I survived with nary a scratch, and chocolate milk and glass in my hair in spite of the fact that a man ran a red light and broadsided us at fifty miles an hour as we headed home from the Dairy Farm Milk Store? Do you want to know that I was standing up in the seat in our brand new Volkswagon Beetle when the car broadsided us? I wore no seat belt, and yes, miracles happen.

  Fear arises, but my mother showed me true grit, human grit as she fought through the tragedy, and demonstrated her Mother-Teresa-like faith as sacred grit: the ability to push through the hard things in life when you feel like giving up.

  Family surrounded us, the church supported us, and faith in Christ sustained us during that time. Of all the strange things I have experienced in my life, I went to my grandmother's house the night of the wreck, saw myself sitting on the curb while an ambulance EMTs loaded my mother in the back of the vehicle, and noted the sun fading near the end of the day as I sat with milk in my hair.

I want to tell you that I write in December. Christmas soon comes. My Christmas tree glows with white lights and at night I like to turn off all the lights in the house and stare at the glowing Christmas tree. Right now, no gifts rest under the tree. The weather outside is frightful, delightful, or however the song goes. It's the most wonderful time of the year, but the weather seems to be cold, rainy, chilly. Clouds hover today.

The weatherwoman reports that today will be "soupy," which means a little fog, a little mist, and large gray clouds floating overhead. I call a gray, cloudy day like today a "Cambridge Day" because it reminds me of Cambridge, England where I have traveled quite a lot to study. On a "Cambridge Day" I usually do my best writing, write in a most productive way, and words flow as easily as taking a stroll across one of the bridges over the River Cam; hence "Cambridge."

Actually, it would be a good day to take a drive in the country in a Volkswagon Beetle or drink chocolate milk or visit a hurting person in the hospital. Did you catch that? You have to face fear by God's grace. Work His grace in you and ask God in His grace to help you overcome fear.

Oh dear, reader, thank you for reading this book. My mother and father appear quite full of happiness that I am writing books. So thank you for reading, and buying, and telling others about this book because, as my dad says, "If you don't work, you don't eat." By the way, if I don't eat, I can't work. Thank you so much for reading. Now where were we?

Did you like the part about the soldier? Did that section make you think of the Roman army and a Roman soldier, or one in a movie or at the airport, or even the name of a soldier in Iraq, Afghanistan, or somewhere in the world this Christmas season? Soldiers possess strength, fortitude, resilience, the ability to hold their own, and the ability to be anti-fragile, that is, to push through the hard things and not give in.

I wrote the soldier section and wondered about Nathan. As a boy Nathan lived in my town, attended a church I pastored, and like any boy played cowboys and Indians and army in his house. The boy grew to be a man and became an American soldier. He wrote me a letter. I

spare you the details in respect of him, and in appreciation of his service to our country, but he did tell me of the hardness, the horrors, and the harshness of war. I sensed loneliness spilled in ink although we were miles apart when I read the letter. I felt sadness as he once wrote me about a friend who died in battle. I touched the garment of sadness and the garment of grief as I read his notes.

I imagined Nathan in fatigues, carrying a gun with a helmet on, wearing army boots, and carrying a backpack full of food and supplies. I imagined Nathan sweating in basic training, climbing ropes, crawling through mud, treading water in a pool, and falling down exhausted after three days of survival training in a remote forest. I imagined Nathan, the tough soldier, a good soldier, shedding a tear as he lay down at night in Baghdad, or in the dusty dessert, or wherever he was. Then low and behold while writing about Nathan and soldiers, that Christmas song *I'll be home for Christmas* by Josh Groban comes on the radio. Have you heard it? I almost cry every time I hear it. A woman comes on: "Honey I love you. Merry Christmas. I'll be home soon." "Mom and dad, I love you." Tell the kids I will be home for Christmas." Soldiers at war in sand send messages of peace on earth and then Josh Groban starts singing, "I'm dreaming tonight of a place I love, more than I usually do...." Come on, Josh Groban, do not make me cry. Every time I hear that song I think of Josh Groban, and I think of Nathan. I think of his courage. I am so proud of Nathan.

I am guessing that Nathan, the good soldier, faces Christmas with fear ("oh heckofa a night"), but finds faith, strength, and God's grace in fear of Christ to push through the hardness and serve too as a good soldier for Christ ("oh holy night!"). Good soldiers face fear with sacred fear, life's fear, with the fear of God, a sacred fear that moves from fear to courage.

Oh, did you like the Sunny Sweeny story? Listening to XM radio one day while driving down the Interstate, Sunny Sweeny, was interviewed by a DJ. She revealed that story, her Facebook post, and the craziness of the picture of the man praying with the soldier at the airport that went viral. I avoid any virus and often wonder how and why stuff goes viral, but loved Sunny's story, and decided to share it with you.

I do not know singer Sunny Sweeny from boxer Sunny Liston nor musician Sunny Sweeny

from KC Royal baseball player Mike Sweeny, but I can tell you "Sweeny" is a German name and means "atrophy" and that, if I heard the radio correctly, Sonny Sweeny's grandfather was/is a preacher. And I can tell you that any singer, or baseball player, or preacher will tell your muscles will atrophy if you do not practice. And I must tell you that your spiritual muscles will atrophy if you do not practice prayer in the hardness of life. Be strong in the grace! Prayer softens the heart to help us handle the hard things, if you can think of it that way.

"Prayer is an effort of the will. After we have entered our secret place and shut the door, the most difficult thing to do is pray. We cannot seem to get our minds into good working order, and the first thing we have to do is fight our wandering thoughts,"[27] writes devotional writer Oswald Chambers. Sacred grit calls for turning our fear over to God in prayer, pushing aside wandering thoughts, worry, and worrisome, negative imaginary thoughts that more than likely will not come

---

27 Oswald Chambers, *My Utmost for His Highest: An Updated Edition in Today's English Langauge* (Garnd Rapids, Michigan: Discovery House, 1935/1992), August 23.

true. Sacred grit demands the prayer of sacred grit:

> "I will extol the Lord at all times;
> his praise will always be on my lips.
> My soul will boast in the Lord;
> let the afflicted hear and rejoice.
> Glorify the Lord with me;
> let us exalt his name together.
> I sought the Lord, and he answered me;
> he delivered me from all my fears.
> Those who look to him are radiant;
> their faces are never covered with shame.
> This poor man called, and the Lord heard him;
> he saved him out of all his troubles.
> The angel of the Lord encamps around those who fear him,
> and he delivers them" (Psalm 34: 1-7, NIV).

The good soldier in Christ Jesus prays in quiet, but also to calm our fears. Walter Wangerin, Jr. writes of a time when faced with a major decision. The decision, like some you make in life, could change the course of his life. It might be a life-changing decision, so to speak. He writes of prayer at a beachside motel by the sea in the midst of the chaos and spiritual battle of the decision: "We were living, it became apparent, in the restlessness like the rush and thunder of wave against the rock."[28] He adds, "Whole prayer grows into the wholeness of the divine relationship."[29]

Circumstances may appear unsacred, but whole prayer drives us to pray in the midst of rush, restlessness, when life seems like the crash of wave against the rock to the Rock, Jesus, who anchors your life in peace, calm, and purpose. Sacred fear looks to God and seeks His face, knowing the harshness of life needs the hardness of God's life in us so we may become a good soldier, fight faithfully the struggle by God's strength, and see God's greater purpose in the end as we grow in relationship to Christ. Sacred grit aims for sacred fear of God in the rush, restlessness, and crashing waves of human fear.

This kind of praying, P. T. Forsyth says in *The Soul of Prayer*, is an act of faith as a child of God and supplies energy in the weariness of life and prayer. He says, "Faith is not simply surrender, but

---

28 Walter Wangerin, Jr., *Whole Prayer: Speaking and Listening to God* (Grand rapids, Micigan: Zondervan, 1998), 22.

29 Wangerin, Jr., Whole Prayer, 206.

adoring surrender, not a mere sense of dependence, but an act of intelligent committal, and the confession of holiness which is able to save, keep, and bless us forever."[30]

Come on, Forsyth, say it more slowly! What did Forsyth mean? Sacred grit leads us not to simple surrender, but to adore Christ more as we surrender. Sacred grit fully commits to God in prayer and life in spite of life's challenges, pain, and trials. Sacred grit in life's valleys carries us in prayer to see God's mountain, His holiness, His sacredness, and His plan even when the light of the shadows in the valley barely breaks through the clouds in a given moment of crisis. Sacred grit believes in God and His light, even when darkness for the moment darkens your sad heart.

Bob Goff put it best in writing in his book *Love Does*, "I used to think that I could shape my circumstances around me, but now I know Jesus uses circumstances to shape me."[31] Goff also says, "Love God, love people, do stuff," but sometimes you have to carry on like a solider and endure

---

30 P. T. Forsyth, *The Soul of Prayer* (Vancouver, British Columbia: Regent College Publishing, 1916/1995), 79.

31 Bob Goff, *Love Does: Discover a Secretly Incredible Life in an Ordinary World* (Nashville: Thomas Nelson, 2012), 31.

hardness to find the grace to love God in a deeper way, people in a Godly way, and do stuff in the simplicity of the sacred. It calls for a holy calling, sacred grit in circumstances conjuring up sacred fear in the eyes of God.

Did you like my snorkeling story about the crater and the green sea turtle? I wondered if I posted that on Facebook if you would like my like of the honu. Do you think I would get one-hundred likes? Do you see that to endure hardness leads us into God's grace to recognize the scared, and that it is a short distance from scared to the sacred? That God affirms us by his grace and shows us grace? That he alone equips us by grace through faith, and by faith through grace to endure hardness and move from fear to courage. Do not be afraid. Do not even be afraid of the broken tooth, the oral surgeon, the big needle, or any needling or trials you experience in life.

The French Roman Catholic archbishop, priest, poet, theologian, and writer François Fénelon (1651-1715) once noted, "Our devotion to God must never stop. We must put it into practice everywhere-in things that we do not like, in things that disturb us, in thing that go against our point of view, our inclinations, our plans. True devotion holds us ready to give everything to God—our well-being, our fortune, our time, our freedom, our life, and our reputation."[32] François Fénelon also said, "The wind is always blowing...but you must hoist your sail." A good soldier allows God to do his part and joins God in his work to do his or her part as a soldier in God's kingdom. The French François Fénelon served as a good soldier.

One final thought on sacred fear as the fear of God in the grace of sacred grit. In my town, news arrived of the death of the medical doctor, former college football star at TCU in Fort Worth, Texas, rancher, soldier, and equestrian. As a medical doctor he cared for his patients and aimed to cure sickness. As a football star he galloped on fields of green on Saturdays in days past as a running back, an all-star, a letterman, a runner up for the Heisman Trophy, and in the sports hall of fame. As a rancher, he loved the land, loved animals, and as in ranching so too in life "he handled setbacks and disappointments with humor, grace, dignity, and courage, and never

---

32 François Fénelon, *Meditations on the Heart of God: Christian Classics* (trans. by Robert J. Edmonson; Brewster, Massachusetts: Paraclete Press, 1997), 11.

once wavered in determination to live his life to the fullest and to continue to be a contributing member of society."³³

As a soldier he fought and served as a medical doctor in Vietnam and received awards: the Bronze Star for merit and heroism and the Purple Heart for those soldiers who in courage served their country in loyalty and were wounded. As an equestrian and a man, he desired, first and foremost, to be a good man and when riding a horse he learned this lesson: "Then always get back on a horse when thrown."³⁴

The man's name was Jim Swink, but I no more know Jim Swink than I know Sunny Sweeney or Bob Goff or François Fénelon. However, he lived as a good soldier. Like any horse-riding equestrian, he knew how to be resilient, to hold his own, and to be anti-fragile, that is, to move from fear to courage and to get back on life's horse even after being thrown. Surprisingly, Timothy had most likely seen this kind of thing in the Roman world, a Roman soldier and equestrian as it was

---

33 "Swink, Sr., James Edward," *Dallas Morning News* (6 December 2014), 6B. Quoted in his obituary.

34 "Swink, Sr., James Edward," *Dallas Morning News* (6 December 2014), 6B. Quoted in his obituary.

called, a soldier riding a horse, then thrown, and then the soldier dusts off and mounts the horse again. A good soldier dismounts and dismays at troubles, but rises by God's grace to live, love, and even laugh again.

    This chapter now ends. I must go home and hang my Christmas lights. Merry Christmas! Be a good soldier in Christ Jesus. And if I have not said that enough or given you enough images of the sea, turtles, rough seas, and dangerous currents, let me ask you to turn the page from Sacred Fear to explore Sacred Agony. As sure as Jim Swink broke rushing records and almost won the Heisman Trophy for the world's best college football player and might have broken a few teeth, rest assured I have set you up for the next chapter. If a soldier guides us in Sacred Fear, an athlete will test our grit in the next chapter on Sacred Agony. I can hardly wait. Merry Christmas and to all a good night, good soldier.

Sacred Agony

From Failure to Success

"It is wonderful after one has tried and failed often-to see how easily and surely the artist is able to produce every effect of light and shade, of sunshine and shadow, of distance or nearness, simply by expressing justly the relations between the different planes and surfaces he is dealing with. We think this is founded upon a sense of proportion, trained no doubt by practice..."

~Winston S. Churchill, Painting as a Pastime[35]

---

35 Winston S. Churchill, *Painting as a Pastime* (London: Unicorn Press, 1932), 58-9.

"You might like picnics with baskets and fried chicken on sunny days when the sun shines high and life is a breeze, but life ain't no picnic. You gotta get tough!"

You might well expect a coach to shout such instruction to the team while the team runs wind sprints and trains for basketball. I have found in life that toughness comes through experience, that experience comes through both the good and the bad, and the best way to gain experience is to learn by failure, that is, sometimes you have to learn the hard way.

In my sophomore year of high school, I played basketball. I did not wear number nineteen like Don Nelson for the Boston Celtics and Willis Reed for the Knicks. I wore number twenty-one, and our road uniforms outlined royal blue stitched on white jerseys. Our team, because there is no "I" in team as they say, the Raiders, played another high school not too far from home. The scoreboard clock signaled in small light bulbs in red numbers that ten seconds remained in the game. The score showed the Raiders behind by one point.

Our opponent scored, and with about nine seconds to go in the game, our point guard dribbled the ball down the court, looked the defense over, and passed the ball to me. Practice, training, and adrenaline kicked my gear into high-octane, and I caught the ball, dribbled to center court, flashed into the lane past a tall, long-armed center, and rose like Michael Jordan into the lane and toward the basket. I added the part about Michael Jordan, but in truth, I played as a short, quick-footed, long-armed two guard whose job was to score. I was no Michael Jordan, but I think you get the idea. Our team needed one basket, two points to win and one point to tie and enter into overtime. The goal in the pressure of time involved scoring, taking home the prize, and celebrating on the way home as only high school boys know how to do.

    I drove into the lane, rose up in the air past the tall guy, reached for the basket with my right hand, and felt another person under my feet or thighs. The other person moved to cut me, foul me, and send me reeling. I did a half-flip, landed on my back, and thanks to adrenaline, received an "oooh" from the crowd. Helped by teammates, I got up, went to the free throw line, looked at the score with the time almost expired, placed the basketball in my large right hand, and waited. The game was on the line between the lines, and I now stood at the free throw line with a chance to make the heroic basket and send our team home as victors, receivers of the crown of victory.

I toed the line, bent my knees, eyed the hole in the orange basket with a white net as I had been trained, released the first free throw, and missed off the front of the rim. Now having a chance to tie the game, I stepped up to the line again, took the ball in my right hand, thought long and hard about proper shooting form, made the adjustment from the last missed free throw, and shot again. I adjusted a little too much and missed the next shot off of the back of the orange rim.

The blue, white, red, and orange collided in a sea of color confusion, the blues set in, and I walked to the locker room having missed the free throw, lost the game for our team, and drowned in a sea of disappointment.

"Don't get your dauber down," an older man said to me as he came into the locker room after the game. No one said much. No one had to say too much. To not let your dauber down is one man's way of saying, "Move past it. Keep your chin up. There will be another day. Don't let your miss, or momentary mess, destroy your confidence."

For years, I thought the term meant, because my friend went to a college with the Yellow Jacket as a mascot, keep your daubers up so that you can sting 'em like the yellow jacket. A down dauber depresses and delays a response in a critical moment. In truth the word comes from an old English word, Middle English, referring to a painter or plasterer who smears paint and plaster on a wall and used a dauber, or a brush. The painter or plasterer had to hold the dauber or brush up to keep from spilling the paint or plaster on the floor. "Don't let your dauber down" indicates stay ready, prepare and be alert, train for the next time so as not to make a mess. Do not be discouraged.

Sitting in the locker room after the game, my dauber dropped, my spirit descended, and my broken wings drooped. A drooping wing limits a flying saint.

Failure, the feeling of failure, the drooping wings of failure, and the dropping spirit of failure, can make you want to stay in the locker room, hide, and retreat for a season. However, as an athlete, which I claimed to be in my sophomore year, learns to lift his or her dauber, rise up from failure, and fluff the wings to fly again.

Thirty-five years later no one remembers my failure, but I do. Our coach, Ray DeBord, stressed fundamentals, handling the pressure, practice and repetition as the key to basketball success, and discipline in the throes of competing schedules for my time and of competing forces in life. Basketball practice led to basketball success, and daily discipline led to practice that produced success.

At a TCU basketball camp, another coach said, "Practice makes...consistent. Only Jesus was perfect." The late NFL Green bay Packers football coach Vince Lombardi used to say, "Practice does not make perfect. Only perfect practice makes perfect." The late and great UCLA basketball coach, the Wizard of Westwood, Coach John Wooden, said, "Success is a peace of mind which is a direct result of self-satisfaction in knowing you did your best to become the best you are capable of becoming."[36] Wooden spoke of his pyramid to success, which included preparation, loyalty, initiative, alertness, skill, conditioning, team spirit, poise, confidence, and a competitive spirit in the promise of good attitude. He stressed "seeing the little things done well."[37] He also lived by

---

36 John Wooden with Steve Jamison, *My Personal Best: Life Lessons from an All-American Journey* (New York: McGraw-Hill, 2004), 87.

37 John Wooden with Steve Jamison, *My Personal Best: Life Lessons from an All-American Journey*, 105.

a simple rule or code: "Talent is God-given; be humble. Fame is man-given; be thankful. Conceit is self-given; be careful."[38]

John Wooden appears to take a page right out of the New Testament in Paul's Letter to Timothy. Paul speaks of the athlete, the training required to prepare for an athletic event like a race, and the agony of competition. Paul himself admired the grit, the discipline, and the agony of the athlete. You imagine Paul watching a foot race or a boxing match in the ancient Isthmian Games in the town of Corinth, similar the modern summer Olympics.

"Do you not know that in a race all the runners run, but only one gets the prize? Run in such a way as to get the prize. Everyone who competes in the games goes into strict training. They do it to get a crown that will not last; but we do it to get a crown that will last forever. Therefore I do not run like a man running aimlessly; I do not fight like a man beating the air." (1 Corinthians 9:24-27, NIV)

Paul warns of running life's race in vain (Galatians 5:2), of watching for people who suggest

---

38 John Wooden with Steve Jamison, *My Personal Best: Life Lessons from an All-American Journey*, 186.

shortcuts to the Christian life (Galatians 5:7), and against doing less than your best in following Christ (2 Timothy 4:7).

Near the end of his life, Paul's speech flows with athletic metaphors, "I have fought the good fight, I have finished the race, I have kept the faith" (2 Timothy 4:7-8, NIV). Paul knew the athlete, the agony of the race, and the arena.

In both, ancient Greece and ancient Rome, the arena drew crowds to watch sports. The folklore of ancient Greece included races and competitions like the Olympics with the force of words like sacrifice, brutality, victory, crowns of victory, and even victory songs. The furor and competition of ancient Rome included runners, boxers, equestrians, wrestling, javelin throwing, discus, and even an event called *pankration*, a grappling, kick boxing, and wrestling combination bound to fill the air with bloods, guts, and loud groans. If the Greeks sought honor to win the prize, the Romans grappled for garland wreaths in the crowd-pleasing pleasure of victory, brutality, and boasts of bravado in achieving the victory.

In life everything changes and everything stays the same. One year later, after my free throw debacle, our basketball team won a championship after hours of gritty practice, hard work, blood, sweat, and tears. The night of the victory, a victory song played and blared in the arena, *We are the Champions* by British Rock band Queen. Today their anthem still stands as one of the most popular of all time. Has anything changed?

Athletes spend millions of dollars on vitamins, sports drinks, clothing, equipment, training weights, coaches, practice venues, and arenas in the thrill of competition. Has anything changed? One of the most popular sports among young people today hails as the UFC, the cage-fighting, blood-letting, kick-boxing ultimate fighting championship much like the *pankration*, an all (*pan*) out effort by fighters who in strength (*kration*) aim to destroy the opponent until the opponent surrenders, cries out, and gives up. Ultimate fighting has a list of rules listing possible fouls, things not to do in an octagon cage fight. The gruesome fights of the dueling athletes known as the *pankration* listed only two prohibitive rules: no biting and gouging. Combats among the fighters produced gruesome bouts of blood.

Has anything changed? Popular sports fill arenas with fans who love the competition, the hockey fights, the NASCAR car wrecks, the bloody cage fights, the gruesome football collisions, and the pummeling fists of boxers blasting bloody noses in the agony of defeat and victory.

Yesterday is today and today is yesterday, and the Greeks and Romans introduced the athlete as a hero, a god to imitate, and a competitor to cherish in the hearts of the fans in the arena.

The Greek philosopher Plato (c. 429-347 B.C.) saw the athlete as a competitor, like two sides competing for attention, for a prize, or for the crown.[39] The Roman politician, lawyer, and orator Cicero, describes the gladiators in terms likened to an athlete: "Look at gladiators, who are either ruined men or barbarians, what blows they endure! See, how men, who have been well trained, prefer to receive a blow rather than basely avoid it!"[40] Cicero described the gladiatorial battles as violent athletic events in the arena, filled with brute strength, competition, and bloody rage. The Greek historian, biographer, and essayist Plutarch (A. D. 46-c. 122), described an athlete as one who trains, contends, and struggles in politics as an athlete does the same in athletics.[41]

---

39   Plato, *Timaeus* 19.B.

40   Cicero, *Tusculan Disputations* 2.41.

41   Plutarch, *Moral Essays* 495.E.

When an athlete competes for the games, or competition in the arena give meaning to athletic contest in ancient Greek or Roman literature, another word follows closely on its heels: agony. The runner runs the race and agonizes to compete. The boxer who fights with fists agonizes. The athlete competes in agony.

Sacred grit demands sacred agony, the athlete's formula mixed with discipline. Sacred agony first needs a voice that can speak truth, challenge you, and provide nuggets of words that you can recall at crucial times.

In John Grisham's book *Bleachers*, he weaves the story of an old Coach Rake, and one of his former players, Neely Crenshaw. Coach Rake built a football dynasty, grumbled at his players, challenged them, tested their mettle, and even offended a few players. Neely Crenshaw was one player that Coach Rake offended.

Coach Rake lay dying of cancer, and his teams and players gather to swap stories, share memories, and give coach a sweet send off at his funeral. Coach Rake had a history of training his players, working them hard, and speaking fierce truth into them about football, sports, and life. His voice stuck. Coach Rake loved Psalm 23, especially the part about "I will fear no evil," taught his players to live with no fear, and that the "frightened have no place among the victors."⁴² Coach Rake had an unflappable belief in himself, his system, his players, and his God.

Neely nervously speaks, having carried anger, bitterness, and angst against Coach Rake for fourteen years. Coach Rake had called him a lousy player, slapped him, and they scuffled at halftime of a championship game. Neely speaks, forgives, and heals with a speech, his own words spoken to former players in memory of Coach Rake.

Hear John Grisham write of Neely as he finishes his funeral speech: "Coach Rake was not easy to love, and while you're playing you really don't like him. But after you leave, after you venture away from this place, after you've been kicked around a few times, faced some adversity, some failure, been knocked down by life, you soon realize how important Coach Rake is and was. You always hear his voice, to do better, and never quit. You miss that voice."⁴³

---

42   John Grisham, *Bleachers: A Novel* (New York: Doubleday, 2003), 143.

43   Grisham, *Bleachers*, 159.

An athlete needs a voice that lasts for a lifetime. An athlete hears a voice that speaks truth for a lifetime. An athlete relishes a voice that reverberates in the memory at crucial, clutch, crisis-moments in a lifetime. An athlete never forgets the coach's voice.

The Christian athlete hears God's voice speaking truth, challenging, forgiving, and urging the athlete to do better and never quit. Viktor Frankl, an author and psychiatrist, wrote a book *Man's Search for Meaning* out of his brutal experience in a concentration camp at the oppressive hands of the Nazi regime in WWII. Frankl lost loved ones, saw firsthand the terrors of extreme abuse, and survived the horrors to find honor and dignity in life again.

He writes of the necessity of hope in life, encouragement for life, and the value of unavoidable suffering through life. Frankl talks of resiliency, in a sense, that ability to push through hard circumstances. He delivers his personal message of survival, holding his own when hope seemed lost. He talks of rebounding to live again, being anti-fragile, how the winds that extinguish some people's life-candle had blown to fan the flame and strengthen his life-candle.

Frankl writes, "If there is a meaning in life at all, then there must be a meaning in life."[44] Frankl pens the meaning and importance of sacrifice, hope in difficulty, and encouragement as a means of survival. In the dark hour, in the dark heart, in the darkness of death in a concentration camp, Frankl carves solid words, "Encouragement was now more necessary than ever."[45]

The athlete knows a coach's voice and the voice of encouragement. The athlete hears the voice in times of struggle, times of pain, and in times when the will to press on wavers. The servant of God knows God's voice like an athlete hears the coach's. The servant of Christ finds encouragement in God's Word. God speaks. The servant of God fights through the struggle, pain, and agony when the will to press on fades. The Voice gives hope and meaning to life in its moments of hopelessness.

The metaphor for such times the apostle Paul labels as agony. Agony speaks of the runner running the race, competing in the race (I Corinthians 9:25), and agonizing as the muscles burn,

---

44 Viktor E. Frankl, *Man's Search for Meaning* (trans. Ilse Lasch; New York: Simon and Schuster, 1959), 67.

45 Frankl, *Man's Search for Meaning*, 81.

sweat pours down the head, the heart pumping, and the arms and legs pumping as fast as possible. The pumping, the pounding, and the pulsating rhythm of the heart agonizes as the restless soul seeks one moment of calm in the anxiety of agony.

Do you ever feel a sense that life feels like a never-ending contest? Does your life move at a pace so fast that your arms and legs barely keep up? Does life speed like a runner except the runner pulls away from the you you once knew?

Agony abounds. A woman drops the kids off at school in the morning, drives through Starbucks, and walks into work only to find agony waiting at her desk. A man enters the race of corporate, wants to make tons of money, be a success, and ends up neglecting himself, his God, his family, and suddenly finds agony his only companion. A married couple agonizes over staying together or ending together, and agony joins hands, yet spreads through the house like a raging fire. Cancer attacks like a thief, intruding your space in the agony of a midnight home invasion and ransacks your emotions, hopes, and dreams. Death arrives at an unexpected time and you agonize in loneliness. Agony from past sin or present misery stalks the soul, begins to fray your nerves like a blanket unraveling threads, and you wonder if you can keep it together.

Agony condemns your soul even though you know there is no condemnation for those in Christ Jesus, but the agony of self-condemnation might be worse than condemnation itself. Agony imposes its strong will in multiple ways, but its strength leaves you feeling weak, weary, worn down, and wondering if life's race is worth the trouble.

Be strong in the grace in Christ Jesus.

No one carries a sign around his or her neck announcing "agony," but you can sure bet, once agony moves into the soul, Christ Jesus arrives as the only hope for cleaning out the trash and refuse that agony leaves. No individual sings a song of sorrow out loud about internal agony, but the dissonant chords ring disharmony, irritating the soul. No one arrives at a party and introduces agony as an honored guest, but its dishonor can keep you from enjoying the party as much as it can keep you from joy in life itself.

Agony wants you to post a sign, "I quit." Agony wants you to sing your quitting song. Agony wants the party to end with you left to clean up the mess.

Years ago, two hikers decided to hike the Appalachian Trail. The trail winds and climbs and descends for some 2,144 miles from Georgia to Maine, or Maine to Georgia depending on where you start. One veteran hiker and his friend, who run marathons, averaged approximately 35 to 37 miles a day and completed the trail in near record time. The hikers completed the trek in 56 days.

One hiker declared, "I am feeling good, but man, it's a long way to Maine."

Another announced at the end of a tired long day, "My feet are a little sore, but there's not a quitting bone in my body."

High-carbohydrate diets, rub-downs at the end of the day, and rest helped the driven hikers press on and push through the weariness, when obviously, quitting might have been an easier road to travel.

Fifty-six days to complete a marathon matches another high achievement—the heroic feat of Roger Bannister who broke the first sub-four-minute mile on May 6, 1954. The British runner received notable acclaim for his speed as a runner, an athlete, a physician, and academic. He knew the agony of running, of achievement, and of success. However, what drove him to succeed was failure. His failure to win the 1500 meter race in the 1952 Olympics in Helsinki, Finland, a day in which he ran his best and set a British record, motivated him to pursue running the mile in less than four minutes.

Bannister knew agony in training, running, studying to become both a doctor and an academic. He possessed the grit to press on in spite of the agony of failure and the agony of success. Bannister's record only lasted 46 days, but since he was the first to do it, history smiled on his agony of running the race.

Grit pushes us to keep climbing amid weariness, as well as to keep running the race when quitting offers itself as an option. Sacred grit, in the grind of sacred agony, inspires us to push through life's mountains, and to keep running God's race filled with grace, when life beats us down and screams at us to quit, just quit.

Have you ever felt like quitting your job, a degree program in school, a relationship, or an organization once dear to your heart? When I missed the free throw and lost the basketball game for my Raider team my sophomore year, quitting never crossed my mind. In my senior year it crossed my mind to quit one night at the kitchen table in tears, but I pressed on.

Once in stress and distress, I thought about quitting as a pastor. The spiritual and emotional tank of pastors often run out of gas and need time to refill, but many quit before they can refill the tank. In my tenth year of a Ph.D. in Cambridge, England, I thought seriously about quitting. Old coach Vince Lombardi once said, "Winners never quit and quitters never win," but no doubt he never played high school basketball, pastored a church, attempted a Ph.D., climbed the Appalachian Trail, or ran a mile in less than four minutes. If Coach Lombardi stood in your living room I can sure bet he would name the time or times he thought about quitting.

Sacred grit inspires us not to quit, to stay in the race, and to trust the Lord of the race. My senior year I did not quit basketball, even though I experienced disappointment, because I loved the game, my teammates, my coaches, and the challenge of the discipline, whose lessons have served me a lifetime. I did not quit pastoring because of God's call, in spite of the temporary setbacks that in the long run proved short-lived considering the blessings, happiness, joy, and satisfaction I received from shepherding God's beloved people. I did not quit my Ph.D. because I made a promise not to quit to the university, and because my professor kept cheering me as I rounded the last lap of the educational marathon.

Two things I know about you. One, you have or are now thinking of quitting something, someone, or retreating somewhere. Human nature sticks to us all. What serves as personal is often universal, and at times life pushes you to your limits and begs you to quit. Second, you aim for the sacred, desire to live a holy life that pleases Christ, but the race overwhelms you and the agony kills your enthusiasm by setting up obstacles.

Near quitting in basketball, I cried for an hour or so and cried my way out of it. I slept and started back the next day at practice. Simple rest may supply grit to help you rise again. Near quitting as a pastor I returned to God's call and just kept doing what I knew to do like I mentioned in the earlier chapter in this book. Understanding God's call and His purpose in life goes a long way in keeping your sore, weary, aching feet in the race. Prayer and God's Word supply nutrients to help you keep climbing God's mountain.

Near quitting on my Ph.D., I walked throughout Cambridge, talked to God as a friend, and thought of all the hard work and the wish not to disappoint, and that pushed me through. Sacred grit invites us to sacred agony of knowing not every race is easy, but with God's help, and the help of others, we can make it.

One day, when I walked through Cambridge as the sun set over the city and the sun's shadows of spring sparkled in the glistening waters over the River Cam while the birds sang, flowers bloomed, and life breathed deeply, I stumbled into a bookshop. Books piled on shelves set vertically and horizontally, stacked on the floor, and in slender boxes, filled the bookshop with the daunting task of finding just one book.

Life's many options call us to make a selection of just one oftentimes. I found this small, white, paperback book dated and copyrighted on 1939. The book scribbled and spotted with brown smudges showed the title on the cover in red letters: *Letters of Direction: Thoughts on the Spiritual Life from the Letters of the Abbé De Tourville*.

Two sentences stitched together like thread on a coat captured my attention in the introduction: "The development of De Tourville's inner life is hidden from us. We can only guess at the disciplines of the body and soul endured by one who broke down after eight years of intensive pastoral work, and was obliged to spend the remaining twenty-two years of life as an invalid; exercising, in the intervals left by pain and exhaustion, a transforming power on all whom his spirit touched, and never losing his noble optimism, his vigorous interest in human affairs."[46]

Do you ever wonder why you buy a book? Maybe you know the author. Maybe you think the book will help you or entertain you. Maybe you think the book will send you on a journey, like a hiker up a mountain, or on an adventurous race of victory. Maybe the book will keep you from quitting. Who knows why a certain book lands in your hand, except maybe you read the introduction and it strikes you that this is the book! If I could pinpoint my subconscious thought when I bought the book, what arrested my eyes and heart, I believe, was the thought of a pastor worn down and broken down, a pastor who resiliently endured exhaustion and pain to find optimism. Now that, my friends, seems like a story worth exploring, a

---

46 Abbé De Tourville, *Letters of Direction: Thoughts on the Spiritual Life from the Letters of the Abbé De Tourville* (Oxford: Mowbray, 1939), 8.

book worth reading, and printed ink that might send me flying high again!

Yes, I read about Abbé Henri De Tourville, a philosopher, reader of law, and trained in religion. He went to the seminary and served as an ordained priest in Paris, France. If you have to serve as a priest, picture postcard perfect and picturesque Paris on the Seine River seems as good as any to throw down your roots and spread the seeds of the Gospel, except that before long De Tourville's tour faded, fizzed out, and he resigned.

He retreated the city and lived in the countryside, alternating between a castle and a friend's country manor. "Foxes have holes and birds of the air have nests, but the Son of Man has no place to lay his head," Jesus said (Matthew 8:20, NIV). Foxes and birds had homes, but De Tourville had no home for his head, but a vagabond tossed back and forth from castle to manor. His heart began to feel the spirit's wind like a fox's tail blown by the wind, and his soul began to sing and rise like a chanting bird in flight. De Tourville wrote training letters, letters to direct the soul, and love letters inviting weary travelers to rest in God's love.

He started by saying, in essence, "Be strong in God's grace. Be a good soldier." He wrote, "Every

day I realize more and more fully that life is a battle; a real battle. But also that God Himself gives His soldiers courage and a love of their calling."[47] Next De Tourville sounded like a coach instructing a runner to keep an eye on the prize or the ribbon at the end of the race. He said, "The soul gains very little from looking at itself. Such an occupation gives rise only to discouragement, preoccupation, distress, uncertainty, and illusion. Looking to the Lord, on the contrary, does us good, and we are gradually transfigured by His personality and by the spirit of imitation."[48]

Makes you wonder if De Tourville looked through a castle window and saw a runner below, or through a manor window to see a jogger, winded and struggling, trying to clear his head, fix his eyes, and keep jogging. Makes you wonder if he rewrote Hebrews, with an eye toward the arena and an eye toward the heavens, "Therefore, since we are surrounded by such a great cloud of witnesses, let us throw off everything that hinders and the sin that so easily entangles, and let us run with perseverance the race marked out for us. Let us fix our eyes on Jesus, the author and perfecter

---

47   De Tourville, *Letters of Direction*, 17.
48   De Tourville, *Letters of Direction*, 68-9.

of our faith, who for the joy set before him endured the cross, scorning its shame, and sat down at the right hand of the throne of God. Consider him who endured such opposition from sinful men, so that you will not grow weary and lose heart" (Hebrews 12:1-3, NIV). Makes you wonder if the exhausted, broken down, and pained De Tourville wrote from experience, and weather he had been reading your e-mail.

Do you ever feel like quitting? If the best experience shared gives fragrance in the flower of the worst experience experienced, what De Tourville experienced spoke to my heart, and his message wafted the hopeful fragrance of Christ on a day when my flower almost wilted.

De Tourville whispers, "Say to yourself very often about everything that happens, 'God loves me! What joy!'"[49] God can carry us through hardness, harshness, the exhaustion and pain in the agony of life's race. Oh, yes, say to yourself; shout it from castle halls and manor walls, "God loves me! What joy!" Shout it on days when the race wearies the bones, when the race pounds the body, and when you feel like giving up. Sing it

---

49 De Tourville, *Letters of Direction*, 83.

when life's music fades and you long to sing the quitting song: "God loves me! What joy!"

What the castle-writing and manor God-joy-loving De Tourville said next arrested my senses and spurred me to run the race harder in renewed strength by God's grace: "I have constantly experienced that in my own case, the most diverse and unforeseen circumstances, I have found our Lord always providing, in the nick of time, that which is best for the training of the soul."[50]

The Lord provides! The Lord loves us to love others, and hurts us to heal us, to serve others. God breaks our spirits to lift our spirits, to humbly renew us, and this becomes a part of the mountain we have to climb, and the path we have to travel in life's race. However, if we do not train daily for the race, we will less likely be prepared when the mountain gets steep, the race swells in the gut with agony, or we have been pressed to the limits. We train in Christ like an athlete, to help us exceed our own limits and trust God. God's strength is made complete in your weakness; His grace supplies strength to press on. God, the head coach, speaks by his voice to the player, the player

---

50 De Tourville, *Letters of Direction*, 76.

listens, and one day the player becomes an assistant coach helping other in the race of faith.

But did you see what is best is for the training of the soul? An athlete trains for the race, for the most critical time in the race, and for the final push toward the end of the race. Training for the race requires daily discipline. This discipline energizes us when the race seems hard, or when we feel winded and weary. We push through. The discipline helps maintain consistency throughout the race, but especially at the end.

The apostle Paul sits in the arena watching the runner straining in the race and the quest for the prize. He remembers the experience, or maybe, Paul himself, like Roger Bannister, once ran a race, and then he tells Timothy and you and me, no victor's crown comes to the one unwilling to compete and agonize by faith in God and grace according to the rules.

Paul warns the follower of Christ to compete according to the rules, a hint both to train for the race and to run the race according to the regulations set out for it. I would just as soon be sitting in a castle watching moths fly around candle light, or in a manor listening to birds sing beyond the window sill, as I would trying to explain Paul's idea of rules and regulations for the race. But let me try to explain, knowing that scared agony means sometimes for which you simply have to train, begin the race in the arena, and learn by doing.

The Greek philosopher Plato (c. 429-347 B.C.) uses the concepts of *rules* in a legal sense, warning of wild, reckless acts or breaking rules, yet the necessity of keeping the laws established.[51] Following the rules in ancient Greece proved a noble thing. The rules protect us and others in the race, like laws protect citizens. The Jewish historian, aristocrat, priest, and political leader Flavius Josephus (A.D. 37-100), spoke of *rules* in the sense of a code to guide conduct, spiritual laws "for those, on the other hand, who live in accordance with our laws the prize is not silver or gold, no crown of wild olive or of parsley with any such mark of public distinction."[52]

Josephus knew the Jewish Law of Moses as a guide to right living in the right spirit, a code of law that produced good conduct, and knew of the Roman footrace where olive crowns provided glory to winners of the race while fans cheered from the arena. The Stoic philosopher Epictetus

---

51 Plato, *Symposium* 182.A.

52 Josephus, *Against Apion* 2. 217.

(A.D. 55-135) used the idea of *rules* in reference to the athlete. He names the *pankration*, a grappling, kick boxing, and wrestling fighter who strives (*athleo*) lawfully (according to the rules) who faces the fight, pushes through exhaustion, endures the pain, endures hardship, and wins the critical point in the fight because he has trained. He said, "Give me proof, whether you have striven lawfully ('according to the rules'), eaten what is prescribed, taken exercise, heeded your trainer? After that, do you flinch when the time for action arrives?"[53] The grappling, kick-boxing fighter trains to prepare for the fight and prepares before the crisis in the heat of the battle so as to have enough strength to compete in and complete the fight.

The Christian athlete, so to speak, trains to know God, His Word, and His guiding rules for life. The spiritual athlete daily disciplines himself or herself in God's rules for daily conduct for the contest of life, the everyday experiences in life: marriage, work, parenting, job reviews, health crises, connections, collisions, and communications so vital to life itself. The athlete fighting the good fight seeks God's good, and lives by the rules,

---

53 Epictetus, *Discourses* 3.10.8.

within the boundaries of the contest, and according to God's rules so that when the crisis arrives, when life pummels you with blows fist by fist, you can endure hardship, find strength in God's strength and grace, and follow the instruction of God your trainer.

The trainer and training for athletes in days past as well as today served an essential role in success. The *pankration* fighter stuck to a training regimen, a narrowed diet, and a plan in preparation for the duel with an enemy fighter. Like the Roman gladiators whose brute strength, fearless combat techniques, and training regimen set them on a path of high risk, and with a fierce competitive spirit to win a crown, the *pankration* pushed the edges to win a fight. The edges pushed started with training, discipline, and a path set forth before the fight, just as simply as a runner prepared in training before the race.

Today, athletes take vitamin supplements, digest muscle building fibers, hire trainers, run miles, flip huge tires, climb long ropes, scale walls, and push themselves to the limits to train for the prize in football, cage fighting, baseball, hockey, basketball, racing, boxing matches, marathons, pentathlons, and the like. Extreme sports, the high flying bikers and skaters and aerial skiers, take huge risks to aim for the sport prize.

The sophistication of the eye on the prize, and the goal of winning the prize in the Roman world, provide training schools, legal contracts, and dummy practice bouts for gladiators and athletes to prepare for the big fight or the Olympic race. So great was the fanfare and interest in of these athletic events that local postings and placards announced the events in cities all over the Roman world, the soon-coming fight or race, listing competitors with names like Publius or Lucius. ESPN raves as the information source of choice for many today, but apparently the Greeks and Romans had their own version of ESPN about two thousand years ago.

Many athletic competitions in Paul and Timothy's day possessed a festive flair, like attending an NFL football game to watch the Dallas Cowboys at Jerry World, or Cowboys Stadium, or a college game day in Waco at Baylor University. Many athletic competitions felt like a circus spectacle filled with music, emotion, high-octane social expectations (think of horseracing fans at the Kentucky Derby), dramatic competitions with winners and losers, and sudden reversals of fortune where underdogs won and overachievers defeated expected victors. The arena crowds participated by shouting, booing, and even insulting athletes in the competition. The goal, in the fight or the race, was to get to the platform. The platform achieved meant the prize would be received: a laurel crown, typically, but it could also be a metallic crown, olive oil worth money, or prizes like cash prizes in a modern day golf tournament.

Again, Paul must have been in the arena at the Isthmian games after a race when the *high calling* occurred, the calling of the winner to the platform to receive the laurel crown. "To the victor goes the spoils," the old saying goes, but to the winner goes the platform and the crown in a dramatic moment after victory.

Paul held this image in his mind, the *high calling* to the platform after a footrace had been won when he penned these words to the Philippians: "Not that I have already obtained all this, or have already been made perfect, but I press on to take hold of that for which Christ Jesus took hold of me. Brothers, I do not consider myself yet to have taken hold of it. But one thing I do: Forgetting what is behind and straining toward what is ahead, I press on toward the goal to win the prize for which God has called me heavenward in Christ Jesus" (Philippians 3:12-14, NIV).

Sacred grit pushes us to sacred agony for the sake of the prize. Sacred grit agonizes in the combat for the goal and prize of God's high calling. Sacred grit dedicates itself to God's higher plan, his grace, strength, love, and never loses sight of the ultimate goal in spite of difficulty, challenges, fear, agony, or obstacles thrown in your path.

I think back to my basketball days. I played basketball all year round. I trained. I ran bleachers, jumped rope, lifted weights, and played until my feet ached, my purple and bruised body could go no longer, and at times when my chin or arms bled from cuts and scratches from elbows or finger nails from my opponent. In training, our coach blew the whistle while we ran the hated bleachers, up and down, and then around until pouring with sweat and exhausted. In one training event, the coach instructed us to race the person next to us. I raced and fell midway to the top of the bleachers in the gymnasium. When I fell, I cut, bloodied, and bruised my shins. "Get up! Keep going!" the coach yelled. Sacred grit means in the agony of the race we sometimes feel the sharpness, the agony, and the bruises of pain, but we get up and keep going for the sake of the prize.

Be strong in the grace in Christ Jesus, but beware of trying to run the race alone. Train by reading God's Word. Train through prayer. P. T. Forsyth instructs the Christian who has discipline like an athlete in prayer, "Go into your chamber, shut the door, and cultivate the habit of praying audibly. Write prayers and burn them. Formulate your soul. Pay no attention to literary form, only to spiritual reality. Read a passage of scripture and then sit down and turn it into a prayer, written or spoken."[54] He follows, "It (prayer) is an art—this great and creative prayer—this intimate conversation with God."[55]

Henri Nouwen reminds us in his book *Making All Things New* that life moves back and forth between *filled and unfulfilled*, between contentment and discontentment, between pain for the moment and joy forever and a day.[56] Christ can make all things new, even our failures. Nouwen

---

54 P. T. Forsyth, *The Soul of Prayer* (Vancouver, British Columbia: Regent College Publishing, 1916/1995), 73.

55 Forsyth, *The Soul of Prayer*, 81.

56 Henri J. M. Nouwen, *Making All Things New: An Invitation to the Spiritual Life* (San Francisco: Harper and Row, 1981),

reminds us, "What counts is where our hearts are. When we worry we have our hearts in the wrong place."

Nouwen adds, "We will never understand the full ministry of Jesus' richly varied ministry unless we see how many things are rooted in one thing: listening to the Father in the intimacy of perfect love."[57] Prayer means listening to the Father in His perfect love. In training we never move too far from John 3:16 and God's love, nor do we move from the basics of the life, love, cross, death, burial, and resurrection of Christ that supply hope, strength, and grace to press on. Christ went to the extreme in discipline and love for the sake of the cross-crown and for the sake of a crown for you to one day wear when called up in that high calling.

Train by personal, daily, and corporate worship. Value Christ. Value His church. Sing praise. Value the sermon. Value the preacher. Value the community of saints gathered and serving in the body of Christ. Sacred grit trains us to love God and to love people. Train by practicing spiritual disciplines like fasting, meditation, silence before God, and the practice of creating sacred space to

---

57 Nouwen, *Making All Things New*, 50.

shut the world out and focus on Christ.[58] Sacred space and sacred grit lock arms to help you in your pursuit of holiness, in your aim to please God, and in the realities of sacred agony. Sacred agony draws you closer to Christ as you learn to trust him.

Train by looking for the blessings in the agony, the joy in the race, and learn the value of small things appreciated in the journey like faith, hope, love, kindness, and meekness. Be kind. Keep your eye on the prize, but also enjoy the process, the discipline, and the journey before and in the race. "No matter how dreary the weather, inside or outside the car (or the race for that matter), there are daily blessings to be found," says Kathleen Norris.[59] Rejoice in the journey. Rejoice in the agony. Rejoice in the daily blessings. Rejoice in the Lord and his strength.

One final thing, I think back to that awful feeling when I missed the free throw, when my dauber drooped, and my spirit wrestled with failure. In life, failure happens. Failure lasts for a

---

58 John D. Duncan, *Sacred Space* (Fort Worth, Texas: Austin Brothers Publishing, 2014), 17.

59 Kathleen Norris, *The Quotidian Mysteries: Laundry, Liturgy and "Women's Work,"* (New York: Paulist Press, 1998), 19.

brief moment of time, but does not have to last for a lifetime. Failure feels horrible, but requires grittiness, toughness, and resiliency, the grit to hold your own, and strength to be anti-fragile in a fragile world. Following Christ might deliver moments that feel a picnic, that deliver the happiness of a prize achieved, and deliver excitement of a team victory. However, following Christ might make you feel like the *pankration*, a grappling, kick boxing, and wrestling fighter who survives by the skin of his teeth.

God builds spiritual toughness and grittiness in us that we might serve Him by serving others. Sacred agony, in the pulsating rhythms and teeth clenching of sacred grit, gives us strength and grace to carry on.

So, really, all I can say now is, "Don't get your dauber down. Do not lose heart. Greater is He who is in you than he who is in the world." No saint makes the high calling without first seeking God, and along life's race, feeling strong winds against you in the blood, sweat, and tears, and grass stains on your heart, and blood stains in your soul in the agony of the race. No one goes through life untouched by pain.

In my life, one mistake I have habitually made: I have tried to do too many things on my own, in my own (lack of) ingenuity, and in my own strength. The longer I have run the race and the older I get, along with the aches and pains as the race progresses, I understand the need for God's grace, His strength, and the value of the team, the community of Christ. In essence, we need Christ, but we also need each other to train us, help us, and cheer us in the race.

For Paul, *competing by the rules* means trusting God's love and trusting other people in the thrust of God's grace of grace in the kingdom of his love. "Two are better than one, because they have a good return for their work: If one falls down, his friend can help him up. But pity the man who falls and has no one to help him up!" (Ecclesiastes 4:9-10, NIV). "Though one may be overpowered, two can defend themselves. A cord of three strands is not quickly broken" (Ecclesiastes 4:12, NIV). Failure may try to break you, but God, friends, and a community like a cord of three strands is not quickly or easily broken. Do not get your dauber down nor lose heart, neither be afraid to ask for help, for a coach to train you for the race, for a mentor, or for prayer.

Who knows, but how silent prayers spoken in quiet hours, when we feel like quitting, might become silent prayers answered to give us strength to push through, and help us rise to find joy again? Do not try to go at it alone!

Sacred grit calls forth sacred agony: daily discipline in life's race to keep going, keep running, and to keep fighting in spite of the obstacles in front of you. We fail and we fight by God's strength to grow in grace according to God's guidelines and rules. You move from failure to success, not garland and parsley crowns, but victor's crowns awarded by the King, Jesus.

Success, however you define it, means more than a worldly crown, but rather having peace of God, peace of mind, and peace of heart that you have done your best for God's glory. After all, sacred grit aims for God's glory. Sacred agony pushes us toward God's grace. Sacred grit and agony combine to help you push through when you feel like quitting. I for one am glad I did not quit basketball, church, or my Ph.D. Agony finds gratitude in the push and pull of the race in the grace of God. Be kind, yes. Be thankful, yes. Be strong in the grace, yes.

Notes to the Reader

Oh yes reader, did you like my story about failure? Have you ever lost a game for your team? I guess you know that awful feeling of being in the loser's corner in the locker room, and the whispers and gossip. "I guess he can't handle the pressure. I guess she caved to the pressure," the whiners will say. I did not cave to the pressure. I missed the free throw. No one remembers that I missed the free throw. They only remember the person who hits the game-winning shot, Michael Jordan of the NBA Chicago Bulls or Dirk from the Dallas Mavericks. Failure in God's hands and by His grace never proves final. Rise to shoot another free throw another day. Do you like the fact that I am subtly dropping hints of my favorite teams in this chapter?

The Dallas Cowboys defeated the Chicago Bears on a cold Thursday night in Chicago while I was writing this chapter. The next day I took my cell phone and found a video of head coach Jason Garrett celebrating with his team. The hugging, back-slapping, and thrill of victory seemed evident in the locker room. Coach told his Dallas Cowboy team something like, "Great victory. Great job. We showed mental toughness, we'll fight, and closeness as a team. That's what it takes to win in this league (the NFL)." Those were not his exact words, but I like the idea of mental toughness and spiritual toughness as a Christian. I cherish the thought of sacred grit, God's grace in the grit, and the Christian community fighting together, and for each other for God's team.

Did you wonder when I wrote if it was snowing in Chicago at the football game? Do you wonder about the weather now? The famed politician and orator Winston Churchill became a painter to help him handle the stress and agony of politics. His book *Painting as a Pastime* talks about painting on a canvas. It relaxes the nerves by forcing you to use different parts of the brain. Painting calls for a sense of proportion, contrast, vision, and audacity to paint in spite of failure. Churchill wrote, "When I get to heaven I mean to spend a considerable portion of my first million years in painting, and so get to the bottom of the subject."[60] The cover of his book demonstrates his love for painting: a single solitary, red flag flying atop a castle, which is really a country manor with green trees surrounded by a lighter green yard near rolling

---

60 Churchill, *Painting as a Pastime*, 64.

English meadows with purple and blues skies as the sun sets.

By the way, did you like my notes from *Letters of Direction: Thoughts on the Spiritual Life* from the Letters of the Abbé De Tourville? Did you think at first Abbé De Tourville was a lady, like Abby? Abbé means abbot in French, the name for a low-ranking clergyman in the Catholic Church in France.

Think also of Abbé as "father." God is our father and De Tourville lived in exhaustion and pain, but also with great nearness to God, and with a deep sense of his own unworthiness. Did you identify with agony and sacred agony in his *Letters of Direction*? De Tourville wrote in the Letters, "That is why the greatest Saints have always shown the perfect combination of nearness to our Lord on the one hand, and a deep sense of unworthiness and weakness on the other."[61]

In exhaustion or pain, or whether you live in a castle fit for a king or a country manor fit for a feast for a pauper, you can seek God and His holiness, and push through the hard things by His grace, even when you feel like burning down the castle or giving up on the farm.

---

61 De Tourville, *Letters of Direction*, 94.

By the way, in my library, books and articles are scattered on the floor along with Bibles, manuscripts, and magazines. I hold unpublished manuscripts. Anyway, I stepped over the mess on the floor and walked over to pluck De Tourville's Letters from the shelf, and noticed a book by Max DePree titled *Leading Without Power: Finding Hope in Serving Community*. I stepped over my mess and stumbled upon DePree's words: "In every church in Celtic Britain and Ireland a fire was kept burning as a sign of God's presence."[62]

I like the idea of God's presence burning in churches as much as I like the idea of God's presence, His grace burning inside of you. Let's start a Celtic movement, fire in churches, God's presence afresh in churches, and God's presence burning in you to produce holiness, sacred agony inspired by sacred grit. I wonder how Churchill would paint Celtic churches with perpetual fire?

Now where was I? We spoke of the snow in Chicago, and my writer friend Hemingway tells me I should tell you about the weather. Oh my goodness! Churchill, the master of contrast in speech and painting, would paint this beautifully.

---

62 Max DePree, *Leading Without Power: Finding Hope in Serving Community* (San Francisco, California: Josey-Bass, 1997), 179

Rain fell earlier today, but the sun peeked through the clouds and whisked around the gray puffy, floating clouds, and winked at the purple sky, and spit rays of sun right in my eye. Churchill obviously has started painting in heaven for the first million years, but if he painted the sun spitting through the clouds and the orange and purple sky with colorful contrast, he would paint a picture that tells a thousand words or sells for a thousand dollars.

The sunset paints a gorgeous hue, but the weatherwoman said last night, "This weekend when you do your Christmas shopping, do not forget your umbrella. You will definitely need an umbrella." The weatherwoman wore a dress and used the word "definitely" way too many times, but I am prepared for whatever weather the weather brings. It's almost Christmas, and I, for one, am hoping for snow falling like Wolf Creek in Colorado where they advertise for skiers, "The most snow in Colorado." I wish this Christmas for enough snow to sled, or sleep all day, or track indented feet of reindeer hoofs on the roof of my house. Let it snow!

Oh, I must tell you, though, the whole thought of rain and an umbrella makes my mind drift back to the fact that I carry an umbrella in my car, and one cold December day two years ago at Christmas I was in Cambridge. I walked through the garden, The Backs, as the locals call it, near the River Cam. While walking on a trail in view of King's College and two grazing cows, I turned to walk over a bridge over the River Cam, and into town to peruse the Cambridge University Bookstore, and grab a bite to eat at my favorite restaurant at the Agora at The Copper Kettle. The people treat me well there, and I can get a table by the window, and people watch and glance at the weather. The food tastes good, too.

As soon as I stepped onto the bridge, rain began to pour, the heavy rains that we call here in Texas, "It's raining cats and dogs!" Punters below the bridge on the river in a boat-like gondola full of passengers unanimously and simultaneously pulled out their umbrellas and covered the boat so that it looked like a bunch of black umbrellas floating down the river in the driving rain. So eye-catching and wonderful it was, I took a picture with my cell phone. If you were here now I would show you the picture. I stood on the bridge, took the picture as rainwater dripped off of my nose, and delight tickled my heart with wonder. It made me wonder why I do not play in the rain more often.

Give thanks for the little things because, if you are not careful, grit takes over and steals the sacred, and you miss the sacred rain or sacred grit of God's grace in the small things. I have forgotten ten million Greek words from my Ph.D., but I will never forget that wondrous day in the driving rain while my nose dripped, my heart leapt, and umbrellas pretended to float on the river in the pouring rain. Do not let the rainy days and Mondays get you down the old song goes, and it's true.

Cambridge never bores me. Some tourist told me a story about the night climbers of Cambridge in days past. The guy told me the story how night climbers climbed the tall steeple at King's College and put an umbrella at the top. The university president was incensed and spent a great sum of money to have the umbrella removed. Once removed by an expensive and huge crane, the umbrella returned to the tall spire the next morning. He laughed when he told the story like he was a night climber and umbrella expert, but his laughter reminded me of Santa Claus and his story made me chuckle, too. I found myself snickering at the thought of university students climbing the spire at night all in the name of placing an umbrella at the top on a night with a full moon.

The guy pointed to the steeple and spire. "Do you see the spikes?" he asked. "After the university president hired someone to take down the umbrella a second time, he had spikes placed there so that no one could climb that high and put an umbrella as a college prank," the informative tourist said.

I found a book, *The Night Climbers of Cambridge* that told about actual night climbers and their escapades. The book begins, "Although it is impossible to write a history of night climbing because there is no such history—the game of roof climbing remains the same, changing scarcely, if at all, from generation to generation."[63] The book showed eerie pictures of ghost-like creatures climbing drain pipes, the side of building, and rooftops at night. While the book did not explain what happened if the police caught you, all I could think of was the risk, the adventure, and the resiliency it must have taken to fall down and climb up again.

---

63 Whipplesmith, *The Night Climbers of Cambridge* (Cambridge: Olenader Press, 1937/2010), 1.

Speaking of risk, another day when the sun peaked through the clouds after a light rain in Cambridge, a group of young men and women at one of the bridges over the River Cam shouted at a boy on a bridge rail. "Go ahead. Don't be a chicken! Go ahead," they shouted and egged him on.

The crowd, the noise, and the boy in a hat on a bicycle leaning against a red brick building attached to the bridge arrested my attention. Then as quick as a bird diving suddenly for a fish in the ocean, he pushed away from the red brick wall and hopped, literally, on the bike and rode across the bridge's thin rail with the bold confidence of a Roman Emperor like Nero riding his chariot into Rome in a triumph of cheers and applause. I watched. He rode to the other side of the bridge and jumped down in one motion. The crowd cheered and applauded. I wondered what would have happened if he had fallen into the river or onto the sidewalk by the bridge. I also wondered if his mother would have been proud, and how do you train for such a feat?

Sacred agony requires training, but like the risk-taking night climbers and bridge bikers, sometimes sacred agony means you have to muster sacred grit to ask God to do the impossible.

You cannot be afraid to fail. You cannot dismiss the training, toil, blood, sweat, and tears. Hikers and climbers climb mountains. Night climbers scale walls and pipe drains. Technicians climb ladders. Bikers climb rails and sail across bridges. If you think about the risk in the race or the combat of the wrestling match of the competition of life, you will more than likely stumble, fall down the wall, or fall off the bridge.

I missed the free throw at the critical moment of the basketball game, not because I had not trained, but because in my subconscious I must have thought of missing the free throw and losing the game rather than on making the free throw and winning the game. Do not fear the risks.

Did you like the story about runner Roger Bannister? Let me tell you this secret. Raider Coach Ray DeBord made me, and the team, sit in the locker room on hard, wooden benches and visualize victory and greatness while listening to tapes about runner Roger Bannister's heroic feats on feet. Coach Ray DeBord talked about Bannister like he was his cousin, and I can still hear the voice of coach, his speeches, and his scolding.

One day my eyes rolled in the back of my head, and I almost fell asleep after two hours of motivational words. "Don't go to sleep on me," he said, as he called me by name. Embarrassed, I sat up straight and drank in every word from coach the rest of my high school basketball career. I never lost another game for my team, and as far back as I can remember, I never had a chance to take the game-winning free throw. And I love Coach DeBord. Some days I still hear his voice.

Voices roll around in your memory. Do you remember you coach's voice, or a teacher's, or your mother's, or aunt's, or father's, or friend who died too young who went to heaven to see Jesus and watch Churchill paint? Do you take time to hear God's voice?

The Psalmist says, "The voice of the Lord strikes with flashes of lightning. The voice of the Lord shakes the desert; the Lord shakes the Desert of Kadesh. The voice of the Lord twists the oaks and strips the forests bare. And in his temple all cry, 'Glory'" (Psalm 29:7-9, NIV). The voice of God roars, strikes, speaks, and even twists the oaks. Hear his voice. Shout glory to his grace! Listen to God's voice. Worship him.

Again the Psalmist says, "Come, let us bow down in worship, let us kneel before the Lord our Maker; for he is our God and we are the people of his pasture, the flock under his care. Today, if you hear his voice, do not harden your hearts..." (Ps 95:6-8, NIV). Sacred grit inspires sacred agony and the will to push through, but be careful not to harden your heart. Spiritual toughness flows with tenderness as gentle as a soft, morning rain in Cambridge on a cool, crisp morning. Spiritual toughness flows with the tenderness of God's mercy. Sacred grit feels sacred agony, but thrills in the glory of God's sacred grace.

The Christian life requires discipline. I so much wanted to tell you more about the *pankration*, a grappling, kick boxing, and wrestling fight. Can you imagine the cage fighters of the present day grappling with the *pankration* of the ancient day? Cage fighters and the *pankration* both live by strict diets, by fierce training regimens like soldiers and Marines preparing for war, and by rules to regulate their conduct and battles. Christians, too, need healthy spiritual diets, rooted in God's Word and prayer, daily discipline for training, and rules to guide their Christian conduct in the world. The spiritual diet, discipline, and rules equip them for daily tasks, battles, crisis moments, and help them face the wrestling matches of conflict and race, without ever taking their eyes off of the prize of God's high calling.

Another way to explain sacred grit as sacred agony means not quitting when you feel like giving up: persevere. The guts of the battle or grief in the race can make you want to quit. I thank God daily for the small victories, the little things, and for giving me the grace of strength to press on when I felt like quitting basketball, the church, and my Ph.D. His grace pushed me through, and thank God for the hard lessons, the joys of discipline, and the release of pressure that led to celebration at the end of the accomplishments. Celebrate the joy. Celebrate God's small blessings and the little things. Celebrate the joy of Christ. Persevere in the agony and muster up the grace of God's sacred grit to get through whatever it is you face.

Robin Warren and Barry Marshall spent years enduring grief and ridicule at the hands of their colleagues while finding a cure for ulcers. They later received the Nobel Prize in medicine in 2005 for their discovery of a bacteria, H. pylori, as the cause of an ulcer and antibiotics as the cure. Marshall even took a risk by drinking the bacteria that tasted like swamp water, only to get sick, and then healed by taking antibiotics to prove his point. My point, though, is that the two doctors and researchers persevered and mustered grit to win the day, from 1984 to 2005.[64]

No small thing, or great, generally happens overnight. The book asked a good question, "Why did Marshall have to poison himself to get everyone to believe him?"[65] Occasionally you may be alone in your belief, but press on. Enjoy the grace in the grit of the journey. Press on. A chorus of angels sing, "Emmanuel, God with us," and God with you.

By now you might be crazy, or at least longing for me to talk more about success. After all, in sacred agony you move from agony to success. What is success? Success is following Christ, staying in the race, and keeping your eye on the prize of God's high calling. Success swings our way when we fail, seek God and His righteousness, and ask God in his grace to help you rise again after failure. Success sometimes means climbing, risking it all, and cherishing the little things like rain and umbrellas floating down a river. Success flows from the heart when you agonize and sympathize

---

[64] Adapted from Chip Heath and Dan Heath, *Made to Stick: Why Some Ideas Survive and Others Die* (New York: random House, 2007),130-2.

[65] Heath and Heath, *Made to Stick*, 132.

with the heart of God to share your heart by serving others in their hearts of pain. Success cheers the runner, and one day rides a chariot into the heavenly skies where Jesus reigns, and Churchill paints, and angels sing hallelujahs of joy to the world! Until then, there is no riding to heaven in a chariot. Success serves Jesus in agony and by grit, as it enjoys the grace that God gives. And, finally, His grace as the old hymn goes, is greater than all our sin, and as John the beloved says, "From the fullness of his grace we have all received one blessing after another" (John 1:16, NIV). His blessing is a river washing over you of grace upon grace.

Oh my, it's late here in my office. It's raining outside and my umbrella is in the car. Oh well, embrace the rain, embrace God's grace, and say grace in gratitude for the little things. Or as they said at my grandmother's house in North Carolina at a festive meal, "Pass the biscuits and gravy and somebody say grace." Or as poet Langston Hughes once penned of the rumble of street cars and the swish of rain and rocks and firm roots and mountains and "something strong to put my hands on," sing a song: "Sing, O Lord Jesus! Sing is a strong thing. I heard my mother singing. When life hurt her: Gonna ride in my chariot someday!"[66]

If none of this helps, sing the grace, or give the grace away. Earlier today, a lady asked me for $20.00 for gas at the gas station. She told me her story and begged, and I said no, then said yes. I decided it was Christmas, and God has blessed me large and small, and the best I could do was give her the money, say a prayer, and share the grace.

I sat in my car and a Christmas song came on, and I sang a joyful song of grace. If agony sinks in, your best effort at grit wanes, sing the grace and give the grace away. Life is no picnic. There's no riding to heaven in a chariot until the chariot comes to carry you home. Say the grace. Pass the biscuits. But when you get to heaven one day, then you are gonna ride in your chariot someday, yes, someday. Share the grace and it might just set you sailing and flying high in a whirlwind, like Elijah in a chariot of fire. Keep the fire burning.

So, rest, take a nap, sleep, or turn the page. Next, we explore sacred sweat: moving from faith to fruitfulness. Even as I pen those words, I think of the old movie *Chariots of Fire*. I stood once

---

66 Langston Hughes, *Langston Hughes: Poems* (New York: Alfred A. Knopf, 1994), 63.

under the huge, golden clock at King Edward's Tower depicted in the movie where two runners run around the courtyard at Trinity College in Cambridge. The movie highlighted the life of a runner who carried Scotland's torch, who carried the name Eric Liddel, and ran under the banner of the Name: Jesus. A man from Scotland, an Olympic runner, and later a missionary to China, he ran the race of life to please God. "I believe God made me for a purpose, but he also made me fast! And when I run I feel his pleasure," he said in the movie. I hope that is an exact quote. I dug all around my office to try to find this quote. Where is that yellow lined piece of paper in that white box? And why do I remember one missed free throw and forget the ten million I made? Practice, repetition, and muscle memory is the key to making free throws in the clutch. Practice, repetition, and spiritual memory, seeking God daily, supplies grace for life's race. Grace gives strength when you fail to rise again. Oh, do you hear the rain falling? Do you like the rain? What color is your umbrella?

Sacred Sweat

From Faith to Fruitfulness

"Wouldn't it be nice to burn all the failures of the past year and start clean?" Sandy said. It was, I think, a rhetorical question, but I went scrounging around for pencils and paper. We wrote down things we didn't want to carry with us into the New Year. I filled up one side of the page and started on the other. At the stroke of midnight we let our lists float down into the fire and watched the edges of the paper curl, then ignite. The next

day I raked the gray ashes from the fireplace and dumped them behind the cabin just as a gust of wind rose. The old year went swirling into the clean, white morning. It was a new beginning."

~Sue Monk Kidd, Firstlight[67]

THE CLOSEST I EVER CAME to farming happened in elementary school when asked to place a deep chocolate brown seed in dirt in a Styrofoam cup. I watered the seed and the dirt, placed the white cup in the windowsill so it could drink light, and watched for the explosion of growth as spectacular as a star bursting in space. I farmed, the seed grew. A green sprout bore leaves, and the rest is history.

When I finally made it to college, I learned exactly how a real farmer works, waits, sweats, and anticipates the seed and crop just like I did as I watched seed, dirt, cup, and light deliver a small green sprig in the windowsill. Except, when I made it to college I pastored a country church, and learned the farmer's ways at the hand of a

---

67 Sue Monk Kidd, *Firstlight: The Early Inspirational Writings of Sue Monk Kidd* (New York: Guidepost Books, 2006), 205-6.

farmer's days by a man and mentor named Merle Taylor.

"Preacher," Merle Taylor explained one day, "if you're gonna be a farmer you have to have lots of faith."

When he looked at me through those weathered eyes, squinted beneath his cowboy hat on a sunny day, he must have wondered if I was an alien from outer space. I looked at Merle: He wore Wrangler jeans with a big star on his silver belt buckle with a buttoned shirt that hung out at the back, and cowboy boots covered with dust as if a windstorm had blown through and whipped up dust. Merle looked at me: I wore nice slacks with a button down shirt, and loafers minus the pennies, and had grown up in a suburban town near the big city of Big Dallas.

He watched the weather and determined his day. I read the newspaper and watched TV to determine what to wear for the day. He struck a match to start his fire. I walked to the wall and adjusted the thermostat. If he announced, "Country," then I announced, "City." If his mother raised him on a paper plate, I was raised on a china plate. I think you somewhat get the idea.

One cold December morning, when ice gathered on the windshield and birds gathered on the telephone pole for church, I arrived early at the white boarded church with a green metal roof. I unlocked the church door, walked in with a big coat from the big city and gloves on my hands. Smoke breathed from my nostrils as hot met cold in a chorus of holy fire, and in a chorus of a morning as cold as I can ever remember. I decided I would begin my day of worship with a simple prayer and an act of noble benevolence.

I walked past the old wooden pulpit, stepped up on the pulpit area, and stooped down to turn on the gas on the heater low to the floor and against the wall. God warms the heart and his people warm the church, so on this December day of good tiding and great joy to all people, I turned on the gas, hummed a Christmas carol, and searched for a match. I found the match, walked over to the gas heater, knelt down to find the small hole to insert the match flame, and struck the match, and BOOM! Oh my, Merry Christmas and a Happy New Year and one big flame for the boy from the big city and one small step for man and one giant leap for mankind, and I almost blew up the church.

I preached with singed eyebrows that Sunday, and lived to preach another day. Merle Taylor laughed when I told him what happened. It never occurred to me that all he had to do was look at me and know that I had been close to fire. I hoped he knew I aimed to live in God's holy fire, His cleansing fire, His purifying fire, and His fire that guides, as simply as a pillar of fire and cloud directed God's people through the wildness of the wilderness.

Most notable, though, came the biblical instruction and the biblical distinction one Saturday when Merle taught me about the sheep and the goats. While he weaned his white, scruffy creatures, babies in fact, he separated the animals with great calm and wonderful tenderness like a shepherd.

"I like your sheep," I said to Merle, pretending to appear knowledgeable about all things ranching and farming, about all things shepherd and sheep, about all things dust of the earth and depth of the fields.

As clear as a bell on Christmas morning and as electrifying as that day I almost blew up the church, Merle laughed, looked up at me, smiled a big smile, and said, "Preacher, them's goats."

Sometimes, I learned, it is as hard to tell the sheep from the goats, Merle later explained, as it is to tell the wheat from the tares.

One Saturday one year later, Merle explained he had been out all morning looking for some of his lost sheep. "When one finds a hole in the fence, they all find a hole in the fence. Sheep and goats ain't too smart," he said.

The sheep and goats separated serves as a clear image in Jesus' talk on the final judgment day. Jesus said, "When the Son of Man comes in his glory, and all the angels with him, he will sit on his throne in heavenly glory. All the nations will be gathered before him, and he will separate the people one from another as a shepherd separates the sheep from the goats. He will put the sheep on his right and the goats on his left. Jesus said, 'Then the King will say to those on his right, 'Come, you who are blessed by my Father; take your inheritance, the kingdom prepared for you since the creation of the world. For I was hungry and you gave me something to eat, I was thirsty and you gave me something to drink, I was a stranger and you invited me in, I needed clothes and you clothed me, I was sick and you looked after me,

I was in prison and you came to visit'" (Matthew 25:31-36, NIV).

On a spring day, or a day when I see sheep and goats grazing in fields, I can think of Merle and recall the joy of farming and ranching. I even ponder Merle and discover afresh biblical images: the good shepherd, my sheep hear my voice, sheep knowing the shepherd, the separation of the goats and sheep, and lost sheep that the good shepherd rescues.

Most of all, though, I think of Merle talking about peanut farming, finding rattlesnakes in bales of hay, waiting, watching the crops and the weather in hope of rain, and working like a dog to harvest the crop. Merle stood on the porch and talked about faith in God, faith in God's hand in the crop, and faith in adversity, especially when disease, weevils, or grasshoppers swarmed to assault the crop.

Merle never complained, taught me much about preaching, farming, faith, and faith's fruit. If I grab peanut butter from the cupboard, I am bound to remember Merle the peanut farmer, and remember how close to God's holy fire he seemed as a man of faith. Better yet, I remember Merle as a hard working farmer whose faith inspires me still to this very day.

If the apostle Paul witnessed soldiers (endure hardness!), watched athletes compete in the arena (compete according to the rules!), then surely he watched farmers harvest crops in a season of reaping a bumper crop of joy (work hard farmer!).

Merle once told me, "Sometimes the harvest comes to nothing. Sometimes with the harvest, we get a bumper crop of peanuts. This year's a bumper crop!"

The apostle Paul uses *kopiao* in Greek. The word vibrates with the rhythm of a famer working the fields, kicking up the dust, fighting the elements, planting seeds, waiting, watching, and weathering storms and adversity. The word eliminates ease. The word calibrates the soul like fine tuning the engine of a tractor as one of precision, one of persistence, and one of passion for faith in Christ.

In ancient literature, in the first century *kopiao* indicated weariness from a long journey, mental exhaustion from a hard day's work, and sweat pouring off the face of a farmer working in field on a hot summer day. Imagine taking a thousand mile trip and reaching your destination, say the mountains in Colorado where snow falls and the flakes of snow fall into your eye while you unload the car, and the tiredness you feel. Imagine a single mother working two jobs and raising three children, worn, weary, and exhausted, and falling asleep on the couch watching television after a long day. Imagine a hard working farmer like Merle, sheering sheep in Texas when the weather boils enough to fry an egg on the sidewalk, and feeling the bone-aching pain at the end of the day.

Welcome to the Christian life. When you signed on for grace, you signed on for days when the precision of faith, the persistence of faith, and your passion for faith increase your faith, but also have the potential to wear you down. Sacred grit submits to sacred sweat as the hard working farmer accepts sweat as part of the joy of farming. Be strong in the grace as Paul repeats, asking the Christian like a farmer to reflect on the grace of God in simple things, to remember Christ in his sacrifice, and to respond to God's grace through His unfettered word (2 Timothy 2:6-9). "But God's word is not chained," Paul says as if he were a farmer observing an eagle unchained, in free flight hoisted by the winds on a clear, sunny, spring day (2 Timothy 2:6, NIV).

Maybe this all makes sense: the solider uses chains to capture the enemy; the athlete trains by using chains as ankle weights, arm weights, and chains with weighted balls to lift like a weight lifter or runner preparing for race, weights removed to make the runner feel lighter in the race; the farmer uses chains to retrieve lost sheep or fence in the sheep; but God's word sets you free, unchained, makes you feel lighter when you live by it, and sets you free to dwell and roam in the pasture of God's unfettered grace.

Two things I can guarantee you. First, just like any farmer at the end of a hard day's back-bending, bone-breaking, and mind boggling weariness, scared grit never promises complete ease, no sweat, and all days in the Christian life with ice cream and cake, candy, and roses. Second, sacred grit, in and of itself, suggests sacred sweat. Sacred grit sweats and works toward God's harvest. Sacred grit as sacred sweat taxes the mind, body, and soul, but like Merle Taylor as a mentor to novice farmers, so Christ mentors and mimics our faith by teaching us how to plant seeds, work, and wait on the crop, and harvest the crop in thrills of joy.

I would like to tell you that living the Christian life is as easy as sipping lemonade on the front porch, and eating blueberry pie or strawberry cheesecake on a cool day when there's no work to be done. But I must tell you, the Christian life works you, and works in you, and works stuff out of you. The Christian life wearies you on some days, and pushes you to your limits on other days. The Christian life graces you, but causes you to sweat in the long days of working for the harvest.

So one thing I say, you are not alone. *Emmanuel*, God goes with you. Imagine taking a long journey and reaching your destination, say the mountains in Colorado where snow falls and the flakes of snow fall into your eye while you unload the car and the tiredness you feel. The Bible reminds you, "Be content with what you have, because God has said, 'Never will I leave you; never will I forsake you'" (Hebrews 13:5, NIV). My mind tosses back and forth on this like a tumble weed tossed in an open field by a fierce wind. Never, though, should you for one minute believe that you might not feel alone.

Many times in life, and many times in ministry I have felt all alone. "Alone, alone, all, all alone, Alone on a wide sea! And never a saint took pity on My soul in agony," Samuel Taylor Coleridge (1772-1834) once wrote in his poem *The Rime of the Ancient Mariner*.[68] Was Coleridge thinking of growing up as a clergyman's son, or of leaving Cambridge without a degree, or of scratching out words for a living by ink and quill and candlelight in the stillness and loneliness of night? Had he once traveled the sea, alone, the ship tossed like a coke bottle on the rough seas? Had he felt the aloneness of rejection at the hands of an editor, a woman, or a trusted friend? Had he imagined a boat on the sea, or an albatross alone in circling the air? Had his father or mother died leaving him in grief alone, all, all alone?

Write this down: Sacred grit inspires sacred sweat, but while you are not alone on God's farm, you will probably feel alone. In fact, the German poet Rainer Maria Rilke (1875-1926) writes in his book *Letters to a Young Poet* to his understudy and mentee, "We are unutterably alone, especially in the things most intimate and important to us."[69]

---

68 Samuel Taylor Coleridge, *Coleridge: Poems and Prose* (New York: Alfred A. Knopf, 1997), 30.

69 Rainer Maria Rilke, *Letters to a Young Poet* (trans. Joan M. Burnham: Novato, California: New World Library, 200), 18.

Rilke rolls out wisdom and twists words in wisdom like a farmer unraveling barbed wire to repair the fence. A soldier prepares for battle alone, reviewing procedures, manuals, strategies, and battle plans. An athlete runs sprints, bleachers, practices, and repetitively practices, even to the point of boredom, when agonizing in perspiration to prepare for the race or game or athletic contest. A farmer works alone in the field, turns the dirt, plants the seed, watches the weather, prays for rain, and gathers the harvest, essentially alone.

The Christian life requires sacred grit in the anguish of sacred sweat that seeks God alone. Jesus said, "But seek first his kingdom and his righteousness, and all these things will be given to you as well. Therefore do not worry about tomorrow, for tomorrow will worry about itself. Each day has enough trouble of its own" (Matthew 6:33-34, NIV). Sacred grit sweats in the joy of God's scared grace.

Thomas á Kempis (c. 1380-1471), the son of a blacksmith, who was amystic, monastic priest, and devotional writer on imitating Christ, once prayed, "Oh, how exceedingly necessary is your grace for me, O Lord, to begin that which is good, to continue it, and to perfect it. For without it I can do nothing; but I can do all things in you when your grace strengthens me."[70] Sacred grit sweats, yet finds refreshment in the dew of sacred grace, and in the grace of God, with which we cannot do without, but with which we can do all things.

Do not confuse the feeling of being alone with the truth that you are not alone. Do not expect sacred grit to always keep you in the crowd, or in the limelight, or in the thrust of a multitude of voices shouting praises of your glory and grandeur. Farmers work alone. Christians seek God alone. God may do his best work in you all alone, all alone. Your greatest ministry will take place alone, away from the eyes of watchers, and only in the eyes of God who, for all practical purposes, is the One who matters anyway. Sacred grit employs sacred sweat for the cause of Christ, but God's work in you recalls the death, burial, and resurrection, and the faith, hope, and love of Christ. These combine as grace to strengthen you when you feel weak and alone so that you overcome that alone feeling, and seek God in his righteousness.

---

70 Thomas á Kempis, *Of The Imitation of Christ* (London: Kegan, Paul, Trübner, and Co., 1898),

In the weariness of work, the occasional exhaustion of the spiritual life, and feeling of being alone, remember Jesus' invitation, "Come to me, all you who are weary and burdened, and I will give you rest. Take my yoke upon you and learn from me, for I am gentle and humble in heart, and you will find rest for your souls. For my yoke is easy and my burden is light" (Matthew 11:28-30, NIV). The farming image of the farmer at work driving an ox with a yoke provides the picture of Jesus carrying our burden, lifting the yoke, and even reducing the weight of the yoke by lifting our burdens for us.

Sacred sweat finds rest in God's grace, His sacred rest, and His sacred hand that lifts a heavy burden (1 Peter 5:7). Cast your burdens on the Lord and He will sustain you (Psalm 55:22). You can rest assured that you can cast your burdens on Christ because He cares for you. He will sustain you in the fear, agony, and sweat of life. Do not forget this in the weariness of God's rest and work.

You can never read the Bible without imagining at least the sense of sheep and goats, shepherds and ranchers, and smell the stink of animals like camels, donkeys, sheep, and goats, and taste the grit of sand between your teeth from the dusty, wandering travels of Jacob, Jeremiah, Hosea, John the Baptist, Paul, or Jesus for that matter. Jacob prayed for grace, divided his goats, rams, camels, and donkeys, then wrestled with God, and reconciled with his brother (Genesis 32). Jeremiah preached God's grace as change, "Break up your unplowed (fallow; hard) ground and do not sow among thorns" (Jeremiah 4:3, NIV). Hosea warns of living by your own strength, "Sow for yourselves righteousness, reap the fruit of unfailing love, and break up your unplowed ground; for it is time to seek the Lord, until he comes and showers righteousness on you. But you have planted wickedness, you have reaped evil, you have eaten the fruit of deception. Because you have depended on your own strength…" (Hosea 10:12-13, NIV). John the Baptist thundered grace as repentance, a turning toward God because the kingdom of heaven is at hand, or is serious business.

The tax collector, Matthew, wrote of John the Baptist, his clothes, his ways, his eating habits, and his affinity for all things of earth and heaven for that matter: "John's clothes were made of camel's hair, and he had a leather belt around his waist. His food was locusts and wild honey. People went out to him from Jerusalem and all Judea and the whole region of the Jordan. Confessing their sins, they were baptized by him in the Jordan River" (Matthew 3:4-6, NIV).

The apostle Paul talked of sowing and reaping, receiving and giving, and God as the sower of seeds who gives blessings: "Now he who supplies seed to the sower and bread for food will also supply and increase your store of seed and will enlarge the harvest of your righteousness. You will be made rich in every way so that you can be generous on every occasion, and through us your generosity will result in thanksgiving to God" (2 Corinthians 9:10-11, NIV).

Jesus washed the disciples' feet for two reasons: to demonstrate humble service; and because their feet stunk, and dust covered them, and sand lodged in between their toes. Grace and grit lead us down paths of holiness that draw us close to God. Agricultural images supply the food for thought and reflection.

The ancient world swirled as an agricultural world, even in both its simplicity and sophistication, because like a farmer, the earth, a good animal, and a plan for putting food on the table proved as necessary as giving the sheep a drink of water. A farmer tills the earth, sows seeds, watches and waters the crop as it grows, and harvests the crop.

The farmer worked hard in ancient days, just as the farmer works hard in this modern day. Merle Taylor worked as hard as a farmer as any person I have ever met. He understood the nuances of farming: working the ground, planting the peanuts, watching the weather, praying for rain, praying against famine, battling beasts like hordes of grasshoppers, watering the crop, waiting in patience for the crop to grow, and harvesting the peanuts. What impressed me about Merle was his ability to do so many things: fix the tractor, repair the fence, chase down wayward goats, drive straight rows in the field, separate the sheep and goats, wean the babies, wash off the mud from the tractor and his boots, harvest the peanuts in a huge cage behind the tractor, deliver the peanuts to the factory, love his family, love the church, talk to God, and love the city boy preacher. He did everything with a sense of precision and determination. He possessed an eye for nature, for broken stuff that needed fixing, and for simple provision sheltered under God's wings spread like the eagle's.

What also impressed me about farmer Merle was his grit, his patience, and his persistence, in spite of obstacles, tragedies, unexpected interruptions, and unforeseen circumstances. In most things he plodded like any good farmer, but never finished a day without giving thanks for God's grace, goodness, and for the small things.

What I noticed about Merle also, was this love for the earth, farming, the dirt and dust, the work minus worry, and the passion for simple things like tractors, wiry trailers, barbed wire, hay bales, a cowboy hat that he always wore to church, boots, an old truck, and the farm littered with animals.

Be strong in God's grace. This strength calls for faith in God, for faith in God's plan, and faith in God's plan for you in the precision (an eye... keep looking to God!), persistence (stay with it!), and passion (this one thing I do!). Precision invites us to trust God and remain faithful to his grace in the little things each new day. Persistence allows us to seek God's grace daily. Passion reminds us of God's grace and love in the hardness, encountering obstacles, and those dry, barren, dust-of-the-earth times that feel more like an awful wilderness than a joyous harvest.

"If you're gonna be a farmer you have to have lots of faith," old Merle Taylor said with his slow tongue and Texas drawl as simply as Farmer Brown asking his help to fetch a pail of water.

The wrinkles on Merle's face beneath the white cowboy hat, the grit between his teeth, and the weathered skin, stood testimony to his hard work, sacred sweat, his true grit. The wrinkles in time, the seriousness of his furled brow on his forehead, and his weathered skin stuck to his gentle heart, testified to his fruitfulness of faith, character, and determination to trust God no matter what. His slow speech, yet gentle speech signaled a warning of occasional danger, homespun-wisdom, and faith that could rescue you from wayward escapes through the fence, from dangerous roads, and pull you out of the mud, muck, and mire of life.

Although I never asked, my guess would be that Merle lived the seraph song of Psalm 40: "I waited patiently for the Lord; he turned to me and heard my cry. He lifted me out of the slimy pit, out of the mud and mire; he set my feet on a rock and gave me a firm place to stand. He put a new song in my mouth, a hymn of praise to our God. Many will see and fear and put their trust in the Lord" (Psalm 40:1-3, NIV).

I do not know if Merle ever cried, but I am sure he experienced enough of the sacred sweat of adventure, danger, the good, bad, and the ugly to cherish sacred grit in the hope of grace, with the joy of seeing a baby calf born on a cold morning, or rescuing a goat from a ravine by the road in the wind draft of passing traffic.

Never did Merle seem more tired than during the harvest when he often slept in church while I preached. Never did he seem more steady, balanced, and unruffled than he did in a crisis. And never did Merle seem happier, more joyous, than when the harvest happened in the excitement of a bumper crop. I do, though, wonder, if ever he felt like calling it a day, or if ever he desired to sell the farm, hang up his boots, and quit. All told, you gotta have lots of faith to farm and to follow Christ!

Jesus told parables about farming, seeds, and his kingdom of grace: "The kingdom of heaven is like a mustard seed, which a man took and planted in his field. Though it is the smallest of all your seeds, yet when it grows, it is the largest of garden plants and becomes a tree, so that the birds of the air come and perch in its branches" (Matthew

13:31-32, NIV). A mustard seed measures about 1.8 millimeters and figures about the size of a pinhead. To live by grace in the large world, you need small faith that pushes you through the hard ground, the tough days, and the days when quitting leaks into your heart like an oil splotch from a tractor on your hand.

C. S. Lewis described faith as "the art of holding on to things your reason has once accepted in spite of your changing moods."[71] He warned of reading the Bible, albeit of following Christ, and missing the obvious glory, goodness, and grace of God. Lewis tells the reader that he is a sheep talking to shepherds, and he likes to bleat. He wrote his first bleat: "They (scholars, readers of Scripture, people of faith in Christ) claim to see fern-seed and can't see an elephant ten yards away in broad daylight."[72]

Embracing the sacred involves slowing down to take in God's glory, goodness, and grace. Embracing faith means walking with Christ and opening your eyes to see Him, how He works, and

---

71 C. S. Lewis, *Mere Christianity* (New York: MacMillan Publishing, 1960; reprint edition, 1952),122.

72 C. S. Lewis, *Fern-Seed and the Elephants and Other Essays on Christianity*, (London: HarperCollins, 1977/1998), 93.

to not miss the obvious joy of His grace. How easy life can trap us, force us into the mud, cause us to be stuck, and we miss the blessings around us because our eyes focus only on the moment of angst, anxiety, or pain. Embracing sacred grit entails sacred sweat that holds on to faith, and hangs on to Christ, in spite of the changing seasons of your life, of your changing circumstances, and of your changing moods.

All it takes for sacred grit to take root is faith the size of a pinhead or a mustard seed, or the size of one tiny cell deep in your heart.

Jesus speaks the importance of the seeds and the soil of the soul in beautiful words as concise as Merle Taylor sharing a tale about a rattlesnake caught in the combine in the harvest of peanuts:

"Listen then to what the parable of the sower means: When anyone hears the message about the kingdom and does not understand it, the evil one comes and snatches away what was sown in his heart. This is the seed sown along the path. The one who received the seed that fell on rocky places is the man who hears the word and at once receives it with joy. But since he has no root, he lasts only a short time. When trouble or persecution comes

because of the word, he quickly falls away. The one who received the seed that fell among the thorns is the man who hears the word, but the worries of this life and the deceitfulness of wealth choke it, making it unfruitful. But the one who received the seed that fell on good soil is the man who hears the word and understands it. He produces a crop, yielding a hundred, sixty or thirty times what was sown" (Matthew 13:18-23, NIV).

The fruitfulness of the soil resonates in the sacred sweat of the farmer's parable.

Jesus then weaves grace and seeds together in another farmer's parable. Jesus spoke:

"For the kingdom of heaven is like a landowner who went out early in the morning to hire men to work in his vineyard. He agreed to pay them a denarius for the day and sent them into his vineyard. About the third hour he went out and saw others standing in the marketplace doing nothing. He told them, 'You also go and work in my vineyard, and I will pay you whatever is right.' So they went.

He went out again about the sixth hour and the ninth hour and did the same thing. About the eleventh hour he went out and found still others

standing around. He asked them, 'Why have you been standing here all day long doing nothing?'

'Because no one has hired us,' they answered. He said to them, 'You also go and work in my vineyard.'

When evening came, the owner of the vineyard said to his foreman, 'Call the workers and pay them their wages, beginning with the last ones hired and going on to the first.'

The workers who were hired about the eleventh hour came and each received a denarius. So when those came who were hired first, they expected to receive more. But each one of them also received a denarius. When they received it, they began to grumble against the landowner. These men who were hired last worked only one hour,' they said, 'and you have made them equal to us who have borne the burden of the work and the heat of the day.' But he answered one of them, 'Friend, I am not being unfair to you. Didn't you agree to work for a denarius? Take your pay and go. I want to give the man who was hired last the same as I gave you. Don't I have the right to do what I want with my own money? Or are you envious because I am generous?'" (Matthew 20:1-15, NIV).

I understand this parable because I worked and perspired one summer in one of the hottest on record here in Texas, 1982. I worked for Mr. Parker at a fence company. He reinforced for me what my father had already taught me: the value of hard work, blood, sweat, and tears. I learned how to dig holes, to mix concrete, to pour concrete, to use a back-breaking and bone-jarring rock bar to bust up rock, how to build chain link and wooden fence, and how to reach my hand out to receive cash pay every Friday.

One Friday I watched, out of the corner of my eye, as a new worker received his pay. He only worked two days. I worked all week, dead-dog tired and bone-weary in the stress and pressure of work. Did my co-worker get more pay than I did? Did he receive the same hourly wage? Did he receive a full week's pay for two days work? Did not my loyalty, dedication, and determination on the job deserve a pay raise, or at least a word of praise meriting an extra dose of bonus money on Friday's payday? These thoughts traveled through my mind as I stood in my steel-toed boots and waited to receive my pay.

Did you see that similar vein running through Jesus' parable of the workers in the vineyard?

"That's not right," a lady whined to me after I shared this parable one Sunday. "They got paid the same. That's just not right, not right." She walked off shaking her head, grimacing at the grit of the story, straining to see fern-seed, but missing the obvious: God, in His grace, gives in generous fashion, not a tight-fisted and stingy God, but an open-handed God who delivers more than we deserve, grace piled upon grace, a harvest of delightful grace, minus a handful of poisonous rattlesnakes.

The parable of the workers in the vineyard drives some people, who search for the sacred, crazy because they imagine that life is always about getting what you deserve. Praise God we do not always get what we deserve! That is called grace. I would much rather feel the joy of God's open hand than sneer in stinginess and the greed of a closed hand hoping no one else receives half as much as I receive.

Beware the hand that bites the giver as much as the hand that hopes the giver does not give and open his hand to another. And beware the hand that refuses grace or the sacred grace that God freely gives. Life sweats at times. Life seeks the sacred. Sacred grit pushes us through the difficulties as we trust God's hand and His grace. Grace, whether it comes at the beginning of the day or the end of the day, at week's beginning or on Friday after a long workweek, as long as it comes, rejoice with joy in the grace that the Giver gives! Rejoice. Rejoice in the Lord. Again I say, "Rejoice!" Sacred sweat's sweet sweepstakes dumps piles of grace into your hand, into your lap, into your heart, God's grace upon grace.

Then Jesus told this parable:

"A man had a fig tree planted in his vineyard, and he went to look for fruit on it, but did not find any. So he said to the man who took care of the vineyard, 'For three years now I've been coming to look for fruit on this fig tree and haven't found any. Cut it down! Why should it use up the soil?'

'Sir,' the man replied, 'leave it alone for one more year, and I'll dig around it and fertilize it. If it bears fruit next year, fine! If not, then cut it down'" (Luke 13:6-9, NIV).

This parable reminds us of God's patience in our work, lack of it, or struggle in it. The parable also points to God's patience as He works in you, through you, and works stuff out of you. God gives time for his servants to grow in Christ. His patience, life's failure, pain, harshness, and hardness, and circumstances work in your soul like fertilizer in soil to supply the right nutrients for you to grow spiritually.

Keep in mind, some people need more time than others. God never rushes, never pushes as if in a hurry, and never forces you along. God, like the farmer, will dig around, aerate your soul, and wait for the fruit to grow a fig, fruit on the vine, or fruit from your life.

My grandmother lived in the mountains of North Carolina in a white A-frame house. She rarely came out of the mountains in her lifetime. She cooked, cleaned house, washed clothes with an old washing machine with a blue rubber roller on top to squeeze water out of the clothes, and farmed. She prayed and had compassion like Mother Teresa who once said, "I am like a little pencil in [God's] hand. He does the thinking. He does the writing. The pencil has only to be used." Mother Teresa also said, "Let every action of mine be something beautiful for God."[73]

My grandmother, whom I call Easter because she was born on Easter and full of the

---

73 Adapted and quotes from Mother Teresa in article: "Seeker of Souls," *Time* (15 September, 1997): 72-84.

Resurrection and the Life, prayed hushed, sweet, whispered prayers. Easter's compassion, and every action, allowed God to write her story and do something beautiful for God. Every soul needs someone in their lives who loves him or her for simply who they are, no strings attached, no drama or wide-eyed expectations, no transferring his or her failed dreams onto your life, and no force-feeding life's theories down your throat like a dog owner trying to force the dog to swallow medicine. Easter blossomed as a flower in the garden, and a fruitful soul in the fruitfulness of her life as something beautiful to God and, I guess, to me.

If one word described Mother Teresa, simplicity would serve as the word. Presidential speech writer Peggy Noonan tells the story of Mother Teresa visiting the White House to receive the *Medal of Freedom* in the Rose Garden in 1985. Noonan writes of her excitement at seeing her, wishing to touch and hold her hand, and Mother Teresa's simple words, "Luff Gott," German meaning, "love God."

Another person tells of arriving at the airport to pick up Mother Teresa and transport her, asking, "Can we walk to the baggage claim and get your luggage?" She silently hoisted a brown paper bag as if to say, "This is it!" She lived a simple life.

"Are you afraid of death," a reporter once asked her. "No I see it all the time," she responded without as much as one light boast of her service to God, to people, to the poor, or of her dying patients for whom she loved as she cared for them and helped them die with dignity. Daily she demonstrated simple love. Noonan wrote of Mother Teresa and her care for the poor and dying, "Her mission was for them and among them, and you have to be a pretty tough character to organize a little universe that exists to help people that other people aren't interested in helping."[74] She demonstrated simple courage, sacred sweat, and sacred grit.

If Mother Teresa called for simplicity of compassion, love, and care for people, Easter lived that simplicity. If Mother Teresa announced beauty in action as the source of love in acts of love, Easter showered the world with love like the fragrance of a flower. If Mother Teresa prayed prayers, Easter prayed them all the more. If Mother Teresa lived a simple life of faith in Christ in Calcutta among the

---

74 Peggy Noonan, "A Combatant in the World," *Time* (15 September, 1997): 84.

poor, Easter lived by faith in Christ poor in spirit, but lived rich in faith, grace, and grit.

Actually, Easter worked the garden. If Mother Teresa wore a nun's headdress, then Easter looked like Mother Teresa in a bonnet in the garden. Easter worked in the garden with a bonnet, wore a dress with an apron, and carried a hoe. I wish I had pictures of Easter in the garden holding that hoe. If I had a picture she would have a slight smile, tired eyes, wrinkles on her forehead, a spirit of joy, holding a hoe next to a white, dirty bucket with a handle, and quietly thanking God each day without many words.

Next to the garden would be another garden: a flower garden flowering and towering an array of colors in spring. "Lead us in prayer and read a Psalm," she would say to me at night when I visited her and my two aunts in that white house in North Carolina. Easter tuned dirt, planted seeds, worked, watched, watered, and waited on the harvest until it came.

She loved the Psalms like these words in song: "The righteous will flourish like a palm tree, they will grow like a cedar of Lebanon; planted in the house of the Lord, they will flourish in the courts of our God. They will still bear fruit in old

age, they will stay fresh and green, proclaiming, 'The Lord is upright; he is my Rock, and there is no wickedness in him.' The Lord reigns, he is robed in majesty; the Lord is robed in majesty and is armed with strength. The world is firmly established; it cannot be moved. Your throne was established long ago; you are from all eternity" (Psalm 92:12-93:2, NIV).

If Mother Teresa had hands that cared for the dying, Easter had hands that worked the garden and a strong belief in God as her Rock, His reign robed in purple majesty, and His strength as a source for everyday work that would bear fruit like a garden. Easter knew calloused hands gripping a hoe in sacred sweat, working, and praying. She also believed in the providence of God's mighty hand. She worked and prayed in the hard times of drought when life seemed dusty and dry. She also thanked God for the abundance and the just-enough in the harvest. She praised God each new day and at the end of the day for his strong hand, His faithfulness, and His goodness. "Give thanks to the Lord, for he is good; his love endures forever" (Psalm 118:1, NIV).

The fruit of the garden that Easter plucked and placed in the bucket proved mouth-watering and delightful to taste: green beans, corn on the cob, potatoes mashed with mayonnaise and milk, cabbage, and okra. Most of it landed on the table in the dining room at evening meals. Any extra food from the harvest she shared with friends, fellow church members, and neighbors in the crook of the curve by the road in the hollow of the mountain next to her.

The fruit of the flower garden blossomed with purple, red, blue, yellow, gold, and green with bumble bees buzzing to suck nectar for building their hives and for passers-by to behold in wonder the beauty of her garden. All eyes saw the garden, knew the sweat of growing a garden, the daily faithfulness it required, the faith of a garden's hope to deliver the goods, and the joy of the garden's harvest fruit.

The fruit of Easter's life multiplied in an array of spiritual hues, more fruitful than the garden, and more colorful than the flowers: "But the fruit of the Spirit is love, joy, peace, patience, kindness, goodness, faithfulness, gentleness and self-control. Against such things there is no law" (Galatians 5:22-24, NIV). This is wisdom that in life God works the soil of your soul, tills the heart, plants seeds, works in you and through you, and

provides over time by simple faith, sweat, toil, pain, blessing, and faithfulness, even when you feel unsure, the joy of fruitfulness, a harvest in you.

I have been on both sides of the garden: in the sweat and work of the soil of my soul being broken, spaded, churned, turned, and tilled when life seemed like a drought, and in the overwhelming joy, when showers of blessing dumped fruitfulness, and the fruit of sweat, work, waiting, and trusting God's hand supplied more than enough.

The apostle Paul, no farmer or gardener himself, but one who knew the anxiety of poverty and the thrill of prosperity, declared the mind of Christ as essential in every endeavor. He said, "I rejoice greatly in the Lord that at last you have renewed your concern for me. Indeed, you have been concerned, but you had no opportunity to show it. I am not saying this because I am in need, for I have learned to be content whatever the circumstances. I know what it is to be in need, and I know what it is to have plenty. I have learned the secret of being content in any and every situation, whether well fed or hungry, whether living in plenty or in want. I can do everything through him who gives me strength" (Philippians 4:10-13, NIV).

So here's the secret I have learned from Merle, Easter, drought, and showers of blessing: God honors faithfulness, and by faith in His hand, your faithfulness bears fruit for God. God does not ask perfection. Jesus alone was perfect. Christ asks that you allow Him to till your soul; garden your heart by seeding and plucking wandering weeds, and through good and bad, find it in you to trust the Good Shepherd to bear fruit in you. You know what the fruit looks like as much as you know what the farm produces and the garden yields: love, joy, peace, patience, kindness, goodness, faithfulness, gentleness and self-control.

If I can return to Merle Taylor separating the sheep from the goats amid laughter, joy, and a lesson in the difference between the sheep and the goats, I return to Merle as a good shepherd, a good rancher as much as Mother Teresa was a good caregiver and Easter was a good, sweet, kindhearted soul who served the Good Shepherd.

The Jewish Rabbi Kushner reminds us that "The Lord is my Shepherd," he provides for His sheep, He restores the sheep, He leads the sheep in righteous paths, carries them through valleys, He anoints the sheep, and by rod and staff comforts the sheep as He leads them to their final destination: the home of the Lord (Psalm 23). Kushner says, "The staff was a symbol of help and support, the rod a symbol of discipline and punishment."[75] The Good Shepherd unveils all that good is, and helps, supports, disciplines, punishes, and guides us to a stronger faith, higher hope, and deeper love.

A shepherd himself, says, "Just as the rod is emblematic of the Word of God, so the staff is symbolic of the Spirit of God. In Christ's dealings with us as individuals, there is the essence of sweetness, the comfort and consolation, the gentle correction brought about by the work of His gracious Spirit."[76] The rod leads the sheep, pointing them in a clear direction, correcting them and protecting them. The staff guides the sheep with kindness and comfort, never forces or drives the sheep, yet rescues them from ravines, briars, rocks, and dangers. The Good Shepherd delivers grace as a gift so the sheep can be strong in the grace.

---

75 Harold S. Kushner, *The Lord is My Shepherd: Healing Wisdom of the Twenty-Third Psalm* (New York: Alfred A. Knopf, 2003), 113.

76 Phillip Keller, *A Shepherd Looks at the Twenty-Third Psalm* (Grand Rapids, Michigan: Zondervan, 1970), 99-100.

The shepherd, as well as the laborer in the field, the farmer, shares and receives first harvest's joys, blessings, and fruits. Paul then says, "Remember Jesus," as if to remind you that Christ's harvest always yields joy, blessing, and hope in the mist and mystery of God's abundant supply of grace. After all, neither God's Word, nor his grace is bound: "God's Word is not bound, chained, fenced in" (2 Timothy 2:9).

In a sense, because God's Word and grace know no limits, this supplies the strength to push through when you feel like giving up; to press on when you feel like laying down; and to cheer up when you feel like throwing up. Paul says it is faithfulness in the belief of God's faithfulness that delivers fruitfulness that can endure (2 Timothy 2:10). You can endure to, even thrive, and show forth God's fruit as sacred sweat, deliver faith that produces a harvest of fruitfulness to the soul's soil: love, joy, peace, patience, kindness, goodness, faithfulness, gentleness, and self-control.

Old Merle Taylor spoke the right words: "Preacher, if you're gonna be a farmer you have to have lots of faith." Novelist Walker Percy once quipped, "To live in the past and future is easy. To

live in the present is like threading a needle."[77] Faith is like threading a needle. Faith means we seek God in the daily stuff and search for the sacred even in troubles.

"Prayer does not mean," said theologian Dietrich Bonhoeffer, "simply to pour out one's heart. It means rather to find the way to God and speak with him whether your heart is full or empty. No man [woman] can do that by himself [herself]. For he [she] needs Jesus Christ."[78] Faith finds the way to God and the way through life by God's hand.

If Merle Taylor proved right about faith, then old Easter sure lived right in quiet hope of work and prayer, prayer and work, caring for the garden, and caring for souls in life's rain, sun, sleet, or snow. I see myself as a young man standing on the porch by the green swing. The flowers bloom and waft a sweet fragrance in the wind. A bumblebee buzzes and circles a yellow flower to find nectar for the day's chores. A car passes by. I wave. Easter works. She lifts her bucket. I hear a light thud as the corn, potatoes she dug up, and fruit fall in the bucket.

---

77 Walker Percy, *Lancelot*.

78 Dietrich Bonhoeffer, *Psalms: The Prayer Book of the Bible* (Minneapolis, Minnesota: Augsburg Fortress, 1970), 9-10.

A gentle breeze blows across my face as I grip the chain on the green swing. She looks at me wearing a bonnet and sweat drips off her nose. God's grace bears fruit so sweet. I can almost hear her saying, "The Lord is my shepherd. God is so good. Some days I think I need a bigger bucket! Trust in the Lord. God's grace and goodness, oh my goodness! Give thanks to the Lord, for he is good; his love endures forever."

Old Wendell Berry, poet and man of the earth himself, whose faith and trust in God's grace revels in words, once penned and summarized what I am trying to say when writing about Sabbath rest in God, a field, its clearing, soil, a song, work, and grace: "Bewildered in our timely dwelling place, Where we arrive by work, we stay by grace."[79] Be strong in the grace, God's grace.

Notes to the Reader

Oh, reader, what do you think. Is grace pouring into your heart like rain splashing down the gutter? Are you tired? Weary? This reminds me of that Langston Hughes poem where he sings, "Hey!...Hey! Weary, Weary, Trouble, pain, Sun's

---

[79] Wendell Berry, *A Timbered Choir: The Sabbath Poems 1979-1997* (New York: Counterpoint, 1998), 59.

gonna shine again someday!"[80] Or where Langston Hughes shouts, "Jesus ain't you tired yet?"[81]

The world wearies people as they pursue their dreams, hopes, and wishes. Nothing materially is wrong with pursuits or the sweat of pursuits, except so many pursue who knows what when the sacred grace of God is what they really need. So many chase something, anything, or everything, or something chases them without them knowing what it is they are digging for or trying to find. In the midst of it all, racial tension, greed, selfishness, sinister games played at church by people who ought to know better, pride, and the dark side of humanity, God must be weary.

The prophet Malachi agreed, "You have wearied the Lord with your words" Malachi 2:17, NIV). God wearies in the world of injustice, hate, selfishness, violence, prideful pursuits, press for power, and the lack of peace. But I have written *Sacred Grit* to offer hope in Christ, trust in God's hand, encouragement for the sweat and weariness of the journey, hope for the broken-hearted, and grace for life's race.

---

80 Langston Hughes, *Langston Hughes: Poems* (New York: Alfred A. Knopf, 1994), 60.

81 Langston Hughes, *Langston Hughes: Poems* (New York: Alfred A. Knopf, 1994), 83.

"Come," supplies the invitation to move in sacred sweat from faith to fruitfulness, "Come to me, all you who are weary and burdened, and I will give you rest," Jesus said (Matthew 11:28-29, NIV). Come weary souls, find renewed strength in the grace of God, cries out the prophet Isaiah, "Do you not know? Have you not heard? The Lord is the everlasting God, the Creator of the ends of the earth. He will not grow tired or weary, and his understanding no one can fathom. He gives strength to the weary and increases the power of the weak. Even youths grow tired and weary, and young men stumble and fall; but those who hope in the Lord will renew their strength. They will soar on wings like eagles; they will run and not grow weary, they will walk and not be faint" (Isa 40:28-31, NIV).

Discover refreshment in the sacred grace of the Savior the prophet Jeremiah proclaims, "The Lord bless you, O righteous dwelling, O sacred mountain. People will live together in Judah and all its towns—farmers and those who move about with their flocks. I will refresh the weary and satisfy the faint" (Jeremiah 31: 23-25, NIV). Do you feel the excitement of grace and hope as I write this? Do you feel my excitement?

While I wrote this chapter I arrived at work early to finish it. When I arrived at work two goats, a mother and her baby, bleated in the back of a truck. The grime on the blue truck caught my attention. The goats, especially the cute baby goat focused my eye. I placed my computer, satchel, and a bag on the ground and walked over to see the goats. Apparently, a cowboy stopped in for breakfast at a nearby restaurant and left his goats in the back of the truck.

"Merry Christmas," a business owner said to me. He saw me holding my cell phone at my office door while looking at the truck and I invited him in to give him a copy of my book *Sacred Space: The Art of Sacred Silence, Sacred Speech, and The Sacred Ear in the Echo of the Still Small Voice of God*. He thanked me. We talked of his world travels. I thanked him for his military service. One thing led to another and we discussed Cambridge. He looked at my pictures on the wall of the bridges over the River Cam, of King's College, and pictures of churches. He referred to me as a man of the cloth, a true gentleman, and a scholar. He saw my volumes upon volumes of books. We both stood under the light of God's grace upon grace.

As he started to leave I said, "I noticed the goats in the truck." He took my picture with the truck and goats. I posted the pictures in Facebook and people made baaaaaaaaaaaaaaad jokes. I posted a comment: "God has a sense of humor. I am writing about the sheep and the goats. This morning I saw two goats...The lesson in writing and life is this: Use what is available; keep your eyes open; behold God's small blessings; give thanks; Jesus is the Good Shepherd. This captured moment will show up in the book. Ha! And Ho! Ho! Ho! Merry Christmas! I hope your Christmas tree and lights are up. If not, call me and I will come help you put them up. Christmas cheer and joy to the world! Have a fabulous day. Psalm 91, Dr. J." See, the post showed up in the book.

"I guess the guy brought his goats to breakfast in his truck," I said to the soldier turned entrepreneur. I hear the breakfast sure tastes good at the restaurant. I have never eaten breakfast there, though. The owner seems nice.

I did not understand what the soldier-entrepreneur said in reply, except I heard the word *cabrito*. I thought *cabrito* might be something you eat. I had heard the word before. I Googled the word: *cabrito* means roasted goat. Christmas

day nears and Christmas will soon be over for the goats. The thought of goats roasted and goat stew and that cute, black baby goat served at a feast or banquet made me sad.

So the goats will not see Christmas or no Christmas for the goats. A simple slit at the goat's throat, the blood starts running, drained, and before long the fire starts. The cook delivers a stake through the goat, the goat rotates on the rotisserie, and the fire flames the goat. The fire cooks the goat, roasts the goat, seasons the goat, and the goat in the field gets served up on a silver platter at a feast at a banquet.

I guess, because Christmas day nears, these goats in the truck made me think of the world in pain. As I write, in Peshawar, Pakistan, families grieve in the loss of their children who were killed by Taliban invaders. In Sydney, Australia, a man enters a restaurant and death drapes over the whole country. I think of funerals of young and old, saints and sinners, and people at the table and those missing from the banqueting table this Christmas. A season of sadness swirls in the air for many this Christmas. Pain and suffering cause some people to only survive the holidays.

Then I think of the goats. I think of Joseph, Mary, and a cast of characters, wise men, the animals like goats, the angels, and the shepherds in their field keeping watch over their flocks by night. Jesus is the Good Shepherd, who as real as the slit of the throat on a goat, felt pain, experienced bruises and wounds for our transgressions, and redeemed the pain through the power of the cross. Yes, I am wondering, too, how I went from talking goats in a truck to Jesus in a manger and on the cross. Did you wonder that? How I went from the manger to the cross, from earth to heaven, from pain to hope, to grace upon grace?

I pray for God's good in the world, and the good of the Good Shepherd. I long for His comfort and healing grace to splash like dew on the earth. I pray for God's light to refresh the earth like morning light, gentle, crisp, fresh, and renewing. I pray for God's grace and light to shine in the corners of the earth and deliver Hope to each heart, even yours, right now.

The Good of the Shepherd in the world of bad overwhelms us with the goodness of His grace and the fruitfulness of His love in the hope of an angelic message: "'Do not be afraid. I bring you good news of great joy that will be for all the

people. Today in the town of David a Savior has been born to you; he is Christ the Lord. This will be a sign to you: You will find a baby wrapped in cloths and lying in a manger.' Suddenly a great company of the heavenly host appeared with the angel, praising God and saying, 'Glory to God in the highest, and on earth peace to men on whom his favor rests'" (Luke 2:10-14, NIV). God's goodness overpowers the darkness still. I believe we have to push through when we feel like giving up to both see God's blessings and to appreciate the wonders of his grace.

Sacred grit as sacred sweat pushes through pain, feels the scar of a wound, yet, remembers Christ who went before you, suffered for you, and will not forsake you.

God wraps his grace, and gives it to you as a gift filled with good tidings, great joy, His glory, and His peace that rest on those who trust His grace.

Have I told you about the weather? Rain falls again, outside my window. This morning, rain awakened me, pattering and splashing on the roof like a child at play. I love rainy days and Mondays, I mean Sundays, especially when it rains and I take a nap. I never miss a nap on Sundays, and I miss Easter and the old house in North Carolina, and the garden. I wish I could take you to that old house. I could talk all day about that house.

I did talk about it, or write about in my book *My Father's House*, based on John 14, "In my Father's house are many rooms..." Here is how I started the book:

Before we walk in the door, I must tell you that the welcome mat reserved for you an invitation to hospitality and good eats, and the right hand of fellowship, communion, and community in an oath, and bond of togetherness. If I grabbed a word out of the sky, I guess I would use the word home. The house, as the song says, felt like home. Home is where the heart is, and for me, was and is and forever will be.

Crazy thing, the house was never my home. I never lived there. I never went to school in the community. I never had my own room, my own bed, or my own space in this house. I never even stayed more than two weeks at a time in that house.

I can name the streets of houses in which I have lived: Algonquin Trail, Shady Meadow, Hurst Boulevard, Souder Street, Shady Grove, Country Lane, Cliff Swallow, and Los Colinas. Yet somehow,

this house on 1415 Roan Road, a road so named because if you follow it on your GPS it will lead you to Roan Mountain where the rhododendrons bloom like roses luscious and pink in the spring, this house worked its way into my soul or I worked this house into my soul as home.

Is home a place where Robert Frost says they have to take you in? Or is home a feeling, the kind you get when you feel all cozy and comfortable? Or is, as Freddy Buechner says, home a safe place, a refuge from the dark, a longing in the flesh, or "that home we long for and belong to is finally where Christ is?" Maybe that is what it was, home, a safe place, a refuge, a longing in the depths of the flesh, a Peace where homelessness and homesickness and trial and error and joy and sorrow and life and death carry you, if not in reality, at least in unreality, to a place of Peace.

In my father's house I am home, but not yet home. The white house with the brown smokehouse down by the creek, and the green porch swing, and an apple tree by the window where red apples fall to the ground, this house was home.

I am a boy arriving at the house in a blue station wagon, sitting in a car seat, looking out of the window and seeing the house while longing in the flesh for the adventure soon to come. I am a boy shaking the branches as Easter quoted a Bible verse and whispered a prayer waiting for the apples to fall. I am a boy sitting in the lap of The Great Unknown, wondering about clay pots and a ladder and the biscuits and gravy with a cereal box in my hands, anxiously yearning for nourishment that only the house could give.

I am a man now, longing for the house and all its memories, power packed and brain fed like the charge a bowl of blueberries gives to the brain, peace-filled and spirit-fed like the peace that settled over and in the house. I am a man, shaking the branches, desiring the delight of a Peace and Light that passes all understanding. I am a man, kneeling in the Face of The Great Unknown longing for fellowship at a table whose delicacies savor the taste buds and remind me to "Taste and see that the Lord is good" (Psalm 34:8).

I think of the house in the mountains. I am a boy, sitting in the green swing on the front porch. An airplane flies overhead. I wonder, yes I wonder with North Carolina writer Thomas Wolfe, "What is it that makes a man willing to sit on top of an enormous Roman candle, such as a Redstone, Atlas, Titus, or Saturn rocket, and wait for someone to light

the fuse?" I think of this house, built by The Great Unknown, and see its white boards and its upside down v-shaped roof, and I smell the mountain air, and I reflect on the past and worry about the future, yet find solace in this home. Yes, taste and see that the Lord is good. Or, let not your heart be troubled. The green swing moves, sways slowly, gingerly. It moves me as it holds my weight and I feel weightless. The rusted chains of the swing creak, and I feel the mountain breeze cool and gentle across my face and feel the adventure like a rocket man in tow, and then I wait, ready for blast off, ready for someone to light the fuse.

That is how I began the book *My Father's House*. God's house, God's grace, and God's sacred joy supply adventure. Maybe if you forget my book at least you will remember the house, Easter, and God's grace in his garden.

Did you like my word on the garden, the shepherd, and Jesus ain't you tired yet? Are you tired yet? Or tired now? Has sweat and work made you feel unsacred? Do you see that sacred sweat in the grace of sacred grit offers sacred faith to help you harvest fruit for better days?

Anne Lamott says, "The garden is one of the two great metaphors for humanity. The other is the river."[82] She also said that you have to face the blank page as a writer, that you will have bad days, that you have to believe in yourself and your art. She adds, "Becoming a writer is about becoming conscious."[83] You write, she was trying to say, from personal story, insights, things that happen to you, and cast light to your reader in the darkness and on your reader's lives as each one seeks to find his or her way. As I write, I try to deliver images, memorable ones like shepherds and gardens, and of people like Merle Taylor and Easter with deep conscious groans on ink supplied even by my deep conscious and the deep unconscious. Maybe the message the writer writes flows from his or her subconscious, too, or maybe, in a sense, from his or her subconscious thoughts, visions, wishes, hopes, or dreams.

Almost finished with his chapter, I fell asleep in bed listening to Christmas music. Bing can sing, Bing Crosby, that is. Bing sang, *White Christmas* and I thought of snow at Christmas. It snowed

---

82 Anne Lamott, *Bird by Bird: Some Instructions on Writing and Life* (New York: Anchor Books, 1995), 77.

83 Anne Lamott, *Bird by Bird: Some Instructions on Writing and Life* (New York: Anchor Books, 1995), 225.

once at Christmas when I was a boy living in Shreveport, Louisiana. I played with my Tonka white Jeep in the snow in coats, gloves, and delight, while snot dripped off my nose. C. S. Lewis tells of a sad, cold, harsh world for many people in *The Lion, The Witch, and the Wardrobe*, a world where "It's always winter, but never Christmas." I fell asleep and dreamed a dream.

Jacob dreamed of ladders ascending and descending in stairwells to heaven. Joseph dreamed of wheat fields and the feet of his brothers kneeling in homage. Gideon dreamed and woke and worshipped God. Job talked of dreams, visions, deep sleep, and the terror of dreams imagined. Ezekiel's head swirled with dreams of whirling wheels, flashes of fire, and sounds as if the chariots of fire in Elijah's day had returned. Daniel interpreted bizarre dreams in historic acts of coming change in politics and world power.

The prophet Joel must have had a startling, mind-boggling, and heart-racing dream when he wrote emphatically, "And afterward, I will pour out my Spirit on all people. Your sons and daughters will prophesy, your old men will dream dreams, your young men will see visions. Even on my servants, both men and women, I will pour out my Spirit in those days. I will show wonders in the heavens and on the earth, blood and fire and billows of smoke. The sun will be turned to darkness and the moon to blood before the coming of the great and dreadful day of the Lord. And everyone who calls on the name of the Lord will be saved" (Joel 2:28-32, NIV).

An angry Herod dreamed. Joseph dreamed and received an angelic message, "Do not be afraid!" The beloved John dreamed on the island of Patmos of lampstands, and bowls, and a crystal lake, and the New Jerusalem, and Jesus (His glory among golden thrones), golden tribes, and golden joys amid the glistening waters of hope fulfilled.

Anyway, I know I am telling you about my dream. I have not forgotten. Beware, because I will interpret the dream for you, too. Beware.

What I think I am trying to say is, I had a dream, and dreams happen, sweet dreams or not so sweet. The dream I dreamed follows:

In my dream, a short woman with black hair sits at a white table. I cannot see her face, but it appears a banquet has ended. Apparently, someone cleared the table of plates, silverware, glasses, food, flower decorations, condiments, and even the table cloth. The woman looks tired, sad, and

weary. She places her head on her arms on the table.

Music plays in the background. The music plays softly, but, honestly, I cannot tell you that Bing Crosby is singing *White Christmas* (Bing can sing!) or Amy Grant singing *Almost There* Or Carrie Underwood belting out in glory *All Is Well* (It's almost Christmas!) or Taylor Swift singing and dancing to *Shake it Off*.

Suddenly, something strange happened. It was the moment I knew trouble loomed, that everything had changed, that all was not safe and sound, and that the person at the table had no place in this world, and that teardrops seemed to be falling like a singer singing and tear drops falling on her guitar. Did you see that? I am telling you about the dream and slipped in titles of Taylor Swift's songs? When sorrow, sadness, and the unsacred arrive at your doorstep, people may wish you to shake it off, but mostly you have to push through by God's grace when weariness, sadness, and circumstances ask you to quit.

In the dream, the lady places her head on her arms on the table. The woman at the table wears red and appears to sleep. She looks dead. The music, swiftly and suddenly, stops playing.

The banquet ends. The party music stops. The fat lady has sung and the opera ended. An eerie quiet silences the dark moment.

Then, almost on cue in the silence, I hear from behind the curtain the sound of a click, clear, loud, and a sound I knew I had heard before. I heard the sound at a wedding. After I performed a wedding ceremony, a couple sang a beautiful wedding song, the song ended, and behind the curtain, off the stage, the sound man clicked off the CD player. He stopped the music. The wedding ended. The music ended. The CD player clicked off. "Wedding over," I thought as the click and the silence entered my ears and everybody clapped.

In my dream I heard that sound again, like the click at the wedding, that same click, that sudden noise behind the curtain. The woman does not move. The lights dim. Then a man wearing a black tie and a suit speaks in the shadows, as if talking to me. I cannot see the man. I cannot tell you if I am in the room in the dream. A man walks over to the woman and does not touch her. Her red coat, the shadows in the room, the white table, and the light reflecting on the stage collide in a moment of confusion, sadness, and deep sorrow.

The man in the black suit says, "I transferred the money. I transferred the money."

The dream ends. The night ends. The music had already stopped. Silence swirled and dust returned to dust. Particles of dust float downward and trickle down highlighted by the light on the stage.

So here is my final thought as an interpretation to the dream: One day the music stops, the opera ends, the party is over, the man behind the curtain clicks the CD player, and someone transfers the money. Until then, know this: Live for God by His grace. Do not sweat life, but sweat as you work and let God work in you and His sacred work bear fruit in you. Your only true currency ("Transfer the money? Transfer the money?") in life is time. Live life to the fullest by grace through faith in the power of God's strong, mighty hand. Trust in the Lord. Be strong in grace. And, finally, remember, like a garden in dry days and fertile days when fruit falls off the stalk, and when it overruns the garden, to always, yes always, "Give thanks to the Lord, for he is good; his love endures forever" (Psalm 118:1, NIV).

His grace gives strength to help you endure. His strength endures forever. In the final click, when the music stops, those who live by His grace will endure forever in the house of the Lord. Sacred grit needs the sacred hand of the Good Shepherd. Trust the Shepherd's heart and hand. The Lord is my Shepherd.

The hour is late. I must go. I am not so sure about my interpretation of my dream, but, really, I must go.

God's grace and peace to you. Grace and peace from God our Father and the Lord Jesus Christ. Be strong in the grace in Christ Jesus. Live, till the soul, work the garden, sweat. Have faith in God, fly like an eagle, shout and sing the grace: "Give thanks to the Lord, for he is good; his love endures forever" (Psalm 118:1, NIV). "Sing to the Lord, for he has done glorious things; let this be known to all the world" (Isaiah 12:5, NIV).

Conclusion

"Oh my soul hangs on thy promises
With face and hands clinging unto thy breast,
Clinging and crying, crying without cease,
Thou art my rock, thou art my rest."

George Herbert, A Poem, "Perseverance"[84]

When I completed the last chapter I entered into a time of rest, Christmas, and travel. I found

---

84 George Herbert, George Herbert: The Complete English Works (ed. Ann Pasternak Slater; London: Alfred A. Knopf, 1995), 337.

myself driving to another city wondering about my past, present, and future. I think we all do this from time to time. Maybe you filter the sands of time like an hourglass through your brain. The past may seem fine or horrific. The present may appear lame or a burden or maybe even mundane, boring, lifeless. The future may set your mind on fire with thoughts of adventure, or might scare you out of your wits inciting fear. As I traveled and traversed time in my mind, I reflected on times I felt like quitting and the timelessness of Christ's desire not to quit on the cross. Many times Christ's endurance inspired me to endure. Many times in life's hardness, weariness, and uncertainty, fixing my eyes, heart, and mind on Christ helped me push through when I wanted to give up.

During the Christmas holidays I went to a movie, *Unbroken*. I mentioned Louis Zamperini in my book *Sacred Space*, but seeing the movie added insight and appreciation for his determination and grit. The gory and gruesome aspects of the WW II military movie, directed by Angelina Jolie, sent my heart in a whole new direction of thinking how gutting through the hard stuff in life can produce amazing, if not miraculous and providential blessings.

I received books for Christmas, one titled *41: A Portrait of My Father* by George W. Bush and another titled *Don't Give Up, Don't Give In: Lessons from an Extraordinary Life* by Louis Zamperini and David Rensin. I will mention Bush's book later. Zamperini's book signals hope for all of us as we grind through the tough parts of life and celebrate the passing of trails in victory. The book also reminds us of four things: 1. We all need faith in Christ for life's gritty moments. 2. We all need help. Louie needed God's help, the help of his brother Pete, the help of his brothers in the military, the prayerful help of his mother, the encouragement of friends and coaches, and the help of God's unseen hand and His inexplicable work in His mysterious movements that we can see looking back, but never see at the time. 3. We all face tough times, albeit not the guts and glory survival of a soldier at sea, or an athlete training for victory, or the hardships of a man trying to overcome post-traumatic stress, or life's stress like a farmer who just lost his crop to a natural disaster like hordes of grasshoppers or thunderous baseball-sized hail. 4. We all need survival instincts, grit in inglorious moments, toughness when the heart screams "Quit! Give it up!" but the will shouts, "Do not quit. Don't give up; Don't give in."

The truth of the matter means that all of us in life face the crossroad between giving up or giving in; between sitting down or moving forward; between crying out in despair while thinking of giving up or crying out in tears of hope while taking baby steps out of the valley of despair.

If you read the Apostle Paul's letters to Timothy you have a sense that Paul instructed Timothy in the ways of Christian virtue, leadership, lifestyle, and commitment. You wonder if maybe Timothy faced hardship, encountered the struggles of both faith and ministry, and felt the weariness of service and conflict. You even wonder if maybe, just maybe, as real as any solider, athlete, farmer, or minister for that matter, maybe Paul wrote to Timothy to both encourage him and keep him from quitting whatever it was he was doing at the time. "Be strong in the grace" provided a simple message. Images of a soldier, athlete, and farmer supplied the illustration for life that easy things are never as easy as they seem, and hard things can produce good things if only you stay in the fight, in the race, or keep planting seeds.

Searching beneath the surface of Paul's letters like ocean treasure hunters mining for gold in a lost ship, we discover Paul's concept of instruction, known in Greek as *paideia*, tutelage at the hands of a personal educator or tutor. Paul uses the word in 2 Timothy 2:16 as a clear indication of instruction in righteousness, especially in reference to God's Word. The word spoke of three simple concepts: training or education; disciplinary correction; and nurture along the path of personal growth and learning; hence a soldier's training, an athlete's instruction and correction for competing, and a farmer's task of nurturing the land and growing the crop. *Paideia* found its roots in the poetry of the ancient Greek epic poet Homer. The word *paideia* in its Greek sense in Homer's poetry indicated educational training whose goal was to produce "a man who was a successful warrior, athlete, singer of songs and huntsman."[85] Greek education as *paideia* aimed to teach loyalty, courage, virtue, toughness, and genuine goodness. The education of *paideia* consisted of mental training in words and grammar often taught through music, of physical training

---

85 Robin Barrow, *Greek and Roman Education* (London: Bristol Classical Press, 1996), 15.

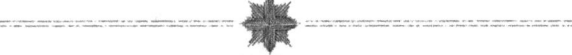

in sports like running, wrestling or the infamous *pankration*, and life skills such as wisdom, rhetoric, logic, philosophy, and public speaking.

Later and into the first century when Paul writes Timothy his letters, the concept of *paideia* had been copied and incorporated into Roman society. It is no small wonder that Paul used these images of a soldier, athlete, and a farmer to encourage Timothy's fortitude and to teach the Christian virtues of patience (stay under the load!) and perseverance (keep going, keep battling, keep running the race, keep planting seeds).

Not long ago I stumbled across a news headline: *Epic Journey Ends in Gratitude*.[86] Keith Lynch traveled 4,000 miles in a canoe from Montana to Dallas along rivers, the Jefferson, the Missouri, the Mississippi, and the Trinity leading into Dallas. The former stock broker lost fifty pounds, met knew friends, experienced wonderful adventure, and in his own words, celebrated the "generosity of complete strangers."[87] The winding journey left him happy, renewed, and relishing the journey's adventure, mystery, surprise of what he called

---

86 Steve Blow, "Epic Journey Ends in Gratitude," *Dallas Morning News* (4 December 2014): 1B, 4B.

87 Steve Blow, "Epic Journey Ends in Gratitude," *Dallas Morning News* (4 December 2014): 1B.

river angels, and longing for home. While some people thought he was crazy, he was determined, and, according to a friend, "that's what kept him going."[88]

If life is a journey, a sacred journey at that, then the faith of adventure, the hope of home, and the love of Christ begs for a determination to press on in spite of daily battles, obstacles, and unforeseen happenings.

If life is anything, or everything, or has any meaning at all, then the search for the sacred will rest in God's peace. The soldier trains and prepares for battle no less packing his or her bag, understanding strategy, and stepping into the war with the armor of God. The athlete trains by discipline, correction, food and diet, and by the challenge of the coach's voice no less to win the race that God gives. The farmer touches earth and dust, and waits for heaven's rain while working his or her fingers to the bone, yet anticipating the joy of God's harvest.

The French scientist, mathematician, inventor, and Christian philosopher Blaise Pascal once opined about *Human Happiness*. He said, "The

---

88 Steve Blow, "Epic Journey Ends in Gratitude," *Dallas Morning News* (4 December 2014): 4B.

eternity of things in themselves or in God must still amaze our brief span of life."[89] Likewise, the things of eternity in themselves or in God should not be missed in their amazement on journeys, in battles, in races, in fields, or in the common everyday events of life. Keep your eyes open, war like a soldier in battle. Keep your heart alive to the wind and joy of the race. Keep your spirit in touch with earth and heaven as you plow and plant seeds in life's garden. Keep going with the dedication of a soldier, the discipline of an athlete, and the determination of a farmer. Keep going by the strength of God's grace.

Sacred grit aims for sacred fear, sacred agony, and sacred sweat that produce courage, success, and fruitfulness. No battle won for the sacred in pursuit of holiness claimed victory apart from resiliency and sacred fear. No race celebrated in reward received the garland crown of victory apart from the spirit of the robust in the realm of sacred agony. "No pain, no gain," the old slogan goes. Yet in the Christian race, agony begets victory and victory births agony, but no victory takes place without sacred agony. No seed planted in expectation

---

[89] Blaise Pascal, *Human Happiness* (trans. A. J. Krailsheimer; London: Penguin Books, 2008), 53.

of an abundant harvest began apart from simple faith in the soil of sacred sweat in anticipation of the joy of the fruit. God invites us to antifragile, a candle not easily extinguished by strong winds.

While writing I stumbled across that canoe journey of 4,000 miles, and life is a journey. Then I stumbled across a story in *Guideposts* about sacred prayer. Writer and spiritual voice Catherine Marshall wrote about her prayer of relinquishment. She wrote about prayer, how she learned to pray through hard experience, surrendering before God a demanding spirit and self-will, and overcoming fear. The prayer of relinquishment supplies God's grace and strength when in fear, agony, and the toil of sweat we trust God and yield to Him in prayer. Did not Jesus pray, "Father, if you are willing, take this cup from me; yet not my will, but yours be done." And did not an angel from heaven appear to him and strengthen him? And did not Jesus being in anguish, in agony, pray more earnestly, and his sweat was like drops of blood falling to the ground? (Luke 22:42-44, NIV). Did not Jesus encounter the sacred by means of the sacred? By means of sacred fear to sacred courage; sacred failure as it were to sacred success in redemption; from sacred faith as he trusted God to fruitfulness in his death, burial, resurrection, and ode to joy?

Catherine Marshall talked the lesson of hardness in the prayer of relinquishment of trusting God even when you cannot see a way out, through, or beyond a given situation. She says, "In God's eyes, fear is evil because it is acting out of lack of trust in him."[90] She adds, "Jesus is saying, admit the possibility of what you fear most. Force yourself to walk up to the fear, look it full in the face-never forgetting that God and his power are still the supreme reality-and the fear evaporates. Drastic? Yes. But it is one way of releasing prayer power into human affairs."[91] The prayer of relinquishment is the courage, agony, and sweat of prayer transformed into trusting God in anticipation of his sacred work in you.

Marshall's word seem drastic, even dramatic, but courageous. Marshall's prayer inspires the confidence to trust God's light even in dark places. Marshall's prayer of relinquishment and challenge to face the fear, made me wonder what it was Timothy feared? Did he fear Roman power,

---

[90] Catherine Marshall, "The Prayer of Relinquishment," *Guideposts* (reprint October 1960; January 2015), 48-51.

[91] Catherine Marshall, "The Prayer of Relinquishment," *Guideposts* (reprint October 1960; January 2015), 51.

government, oppression, and the oiled machinery of organized Roman politics? Did he fear society with its foibles and frailties? Did he fear the church like a ship cruising, at times tossed by winds and storms, and occasionally shipwrecked? Did he fear Paul, longing to please himself, but failing to please? Did he fear failure? Did he fear agony and sweat, hard work in the chariot race of ministry? Did he fear himself? Did he fear failing God himself?

All this fear talk makes me wonder what you fear? Can you muster up an ounce of courage to seek the sacred? Can you pinch an ounce of grit to press on toward succeeding in serving God as you agonize in the sacred? Can you catch a drip of sweat in a cup and show faith the size of a mustard seed in confidence in God as you work and God works in you to till the soil of your soil?

Like my friend Taylor searching for his son in the weariness and numbness of shock, we may find ourselves searching for the sacred in desperation. On the other hand, we might like a soldier, an athlete, or a farmer find ourselves strategically searching for the sacred in the daily course of life. Better yet, we might stumble upon it on a journey like a man in a canoe plodding and paddling while anxiously longing for home.

Keep the eternity of things, and keep the things of eternity in your heart, and learn to keep your eyes and heart open in amazement to the joy of Christ. Life presents a battle. Other days life is like a wrestling match, an obstacle course, and a race where the blood pumps, muscles ache, and the body feels beat. Still other days life is much like a farmer planting seeds, disappointing at worst in a failed harvest, or rejoicing at best in the abundance of rain, crops, and fruit.

Ernest Hemingway gives advice to writers, "I had learned already never to empty the well of my writing, but always to stop when there was still something there in the deep part of the well, and let it refill at night from the springs that fed it."[92] Hemingway may not have been writing to Christians in the battle, in the race, or in the field pointing toward fruit, but his advice speaks to the Christian in quest of the sacred. Essential to the quest of the Christian life to maintain spiritual depth by God's grace and strength, requires daily rest, finding peace in Christ, refilling the spirit like

---

92 Larry W. Phillips, ed., *Ernest Hemingway on Writing* (New York, New York: Scribner, 1984), 43.

a writer or farmer refilling well, and never losing sight of the goal of God's high calling.

The Rule of Saint Benedict written by saint Benedict of Nursia (c. 480-543 or 547), which explores monastic rules for beginning saints and monks, and sage wisdom for those seeking Christ in the sacred in his or her journey, speaks to the formation the sacredness of humility. He wrote in chapter seven, "The fourth step in humility is reached when anyone in the exercise of obedience patiently and with a quiet mind bears all that is inflicted upon him, things contrary to nature and even at times unjust, and in suffering all these he neither wearies nor gives over the work, since the Scripture says, 'But he who stands firm to the end will be saved' (Matt 24:13, NIV); also 'Let your heart be comforted, and expect the Lord.'"[93]

One key element of sacred grit involves grinding through certain parts of life in the notion that God, like a commanding officer, a coach, or an old farmer training a young farmer, seeks to shape and mold your life. He aims for obedience to His voice like obedience to the commanding officer, the coach, or the master farmer. He welds and

---

93 St. Benedict, *The Rule of St. Benedict* (trans. Cardinal Gasquet; Mineola, New York: dover Publications, 2007), 14.

works in you to shape your bravery in battle, your fortitude in the race, and your belief in the fruit of the harvest.

Spiritual writer of the spiritual disciplines Richard Foster follows this path of obedience borrowing from St. Benedict when he says, "A fourth advice in holy obedience is to get up quickly and keep going if you stumble and fall."[94] He warns of trying too hard, trusting God in simplicity, and taking ourselves too seriously. He further remarks, "Joy, not grit, is the hallmark of holy obedience."[95] Joy might serve as the hallmark, the high point, the pinnacle of sacred grit, but nonetheless the grit of battle, of the race, and of sacred sweat provide a path to God's joy.

"Rejoice in the Lord always. I will say it again: Rejoice! Let your gentleness be evident to all. The Lord is near. Do not be anxious about anything, but in everything, by prayer and petition, with thanksgiving, present your requests to God. And the peace of God, which transcends all understanding, will guard your hearts and your minds

---

94 Richard J. Foster, *Freedom of Simplicity* (New York: HarperCollins, 1981), 107.

95 Richard J. Foster, *Freedom of Simplicity* (New York: HarperCollins, 1981), 102.

in Christ Jesus," the Apostle Paul counsels Christians in Philippi (Philippians 4:4-7, NIV).

Sacred grit supplies holiness both because of and in spite of the struggle of the battle, the agony of life's race, and the trails of sowing seeds. In a word, the images of a soldier, an athlete, and a farmer show us that the training, discipline, and challenges persevere toward joy, and are always for our good.

The writer of Hebrews describes this good: "Our fathers disciplined us for a little while as they thought best; but God disciplines us for our good, that we may share in his holiness. No discipline seems pleasant at the time, but painful. Later on, however, it produces a harvest of righteousness and peace for those who have been trained by it. Therefore, strengthen your feeble arms and weak knees. 'Make level paths for your feet,' so that the lame may not be disabled, but rather healed. Make every effort to live in peace with all men and to be holy; without holiness no one will see the Lord" (Hebrews 12:10-15, NIV).

In a strange twist, sacred grit in the shadow and strength of God's grace provides both joy and peace. After war, peace settles. After a race, the peace of victory celebrates the joy of agony worth the effort. After toil and labor in fields of sweat, the farmer finds rest, maybe a long winter's nap, and peace. The task complete, the peace compliments the task. It is always good to remember God's ways are not always our ways, "'For my thoughts are not your thoughts, neither are your ways my ways,' declares the Lord. 'As the heavens are higher than the earth, so are my ways higher than your ways and my thoughts than your thoughts'" (Isaiah 55:8-9, NIV).

While moving books in my office, I found a book that the brown and green of the cover caught my attention. I remembered one day in Cambridge when bored, I wandered into a bookshop and plucked this book off the shelf, purchased I, read it, marked it, and forgot all about it. The book has a title: *The Book of the Shepherd: The Story of One Simple Prayer and How It Changed the World* and offers a simple prayer, "Please father have mercy on me."[96] The book tells the story of a shepherd, a father's mercy, a sacred search, healing that comes through loving, and how one small thing, one small act, one small grain of sand can make a difference. *The Book of the Shepherd* focuses on St.

---

96 The Scribe, *The Book of the Shepherd: The Story of One Simple Prayer and How It Changed the World* (New York: HarperCollins, 2009), 3.

Francis of Assisi's prayer: make me a channel of your peace.

The book ends with a simple message: "Results take time. Hold the vision. Remember the gathering force. Each grain alone seems light and insignificant. Yet one speck can cause the shift."[97] The scribe tells the shepherd's tale that mercy triumphs over judgment, and that compassion fills the world with God's love, so much so that one person can bring change in the world by showing God's love. Showing God's love and sowing seeds of God's love require the sacred grit of God's servants who follow the Good Shepherd.

Understanding and living according to God's love calls for a soldier's sacred courage, an athlete's sacred agony, and a farmer's sacred sweat. *Paideia* and prayer, patience and perseverance, and God's grace and strength pave the way for courage to flourish, service to God to succeed, and faith to bear delightful fruit. You plow in grit and God's delivers the power of his grace.

A cold, damp day pauses as the last day of the year ends. Weather forecasters predict drizzle, gray clouds, and possibly light, freezing rain.

---

97 The Scribe, *The Book of the Shepherd: The Story of One Simple Prayer and How It Changed the World* (New York: HarperCollins, 2009), 165.

Meanwhile, I plow in ink and finish this book. I encourage you to fight the fight of faith by God's grace like a solider. I challenge you to run life's race with God's grace as your supply of strength. I reassure you that life is not always easy, but trudging forward amid the mud, rain, weather, trials, and tribulations of life like a farmer yields results of spiritual fruit and the fruit of joy.

I know. I know. You still wonder if I forgot about President Bush, right? The book *41: A Portrait of My Father* by George W. Bush? Former President George W. Bush tells of his father, former President George H. W. Bush's ninetieth birthday. G. H. W. B. jumped out of a helicopter with a paratrooper and a parachute on his ninetieth birthday. He jumped, came in hot, which means off course, landed on his face on the ground, got up, smiled, and kissed his wife. Mission accomplished!

Before he took off and jumped, his granddaughter asked him, "What's your birthday wish on your ninetieth birthday?"

"For happiness for my grandkids. I hope they have the same kind of life I have for ninety years- full of joy," he replied.[98] He then chimed in after

---

98 George W. Bush, *41: A Portrait of My Father* (New York: Crown Publishers, 2014), 3.

a pause with his wry sense of humor, "Make sure the parachute opens."[99]

In life, sometimes you simply have to jump, to take the leap, to seize the moment, and to celebrate with joy God's grace, His goodness, and His greatness in the pursuit of the sacred in the reality of the grit. You jump into fear, over failure, and into faith's adventure. Joy comes in the adventure of life, even the struggle of the battle. Joy comes through the windswept agony, preparation, and discipline of running life's race with the wind in your face, often against all odds. Joy comes through the daily sweat, toil, labor, and grind that often in the dust leaves the grit in your teeth, but the joy of the journey in your heart.

Did you see that? I am back in the dentist's chair, overcoming fear? I am back at the free throw line, failing to succeed. Did you see that? I am leaving the separation of the sheep and goats in God's hands, but enjoying the land, the earth, the people, and the unseen hand of God, living so I can work for God to His glory, and so that He can work in me to bear His fruit. Did you see that? I am standing midflight, mid-air, waiting for God's

---

99 George W. Bush, *41: A Portrait of My Father* (New York: Crown Publishers, 2014), 3.

cadence call: "Jump! Jump, baby, jump! Fly, baby, fly! Go! Don't stop!"

Sometimes I guess, in the battle, in the race, and in the dusty field, you simply need to grit your teeth, keep going, and seek the sacred in the daily grind beneath the grace of the shadow of the glorious cross. Sacred grit struggles, agonizes, sweats, and then sings a song of joy.

www.ingramcontent.com/pod-product-compliance
Lightning Source LLC
Chambersburg PA
CBHW071701090426
42738CB00009B/1620